D1378419

CHAMBERS of HORROR

CHAMBERS OF HORROR

MONSTROUS CRIMES OF THE MODERN AGE

JOHN MARLOWE

PICTURE CREDITS

Bill Stoneham: 249, 265

Corbis: 51 (Zuma Press/Pat Dollens), 88, 92, 100, 103, 109, 130, 133, 143, 147, 160, 172, 213, 243, 287, 291

Getty: 12, 15, 48, 78, 84, 85

Rex Features: 60 (newspix), 214

PA Photos: 62, 116, 186, 203, 235, 273, 275

Shutterstock: 239

Topfoto: 70, 74, 194, 198, 283

Zuma Press: 45, 184, 219 (Sacramento Bee/Michael Williamson)

This edition published in 2018 by Arcturus Publishing Limited
26/27 Bickels Yard, 151–153 Bermondsey Street,
London SE1 3HA

Copyright © Arcturus Holdings Limited

All rights reserved. No part of this publication may be reproduced, stored in a retrieval system, or transmitted, in any form or by any means, electronic, mechanical, photocopying, recording or otherwise, without prior written permission in accordance with the provisions of the Copyright Act 1956 (as amended). Any person or persons who do any unauthorised act in relation to this publication may be liable to criminal prosecution and civil claims for damages.

AD006187UK

Printed in the UK

CONTENTS

INTRODUCTION

In the middle of the 19th century, a French immigrant to London constructed what she called her 'Chamber of Horrors'. Its contents were both horrific and shocking. Visitors to the room encountered severed heads on stakes, blood-covered victims and menacing murderers whose crimes were so horrendous that their names are remembered even today. Anna Marie Tussaud ('Madame Tussaud') made a great deal of money from this grisly chamber, which capitalized on the public's thirst for the macabre.

Nothing much has changed since that time. The public's fascination with the ghastly and gruesome continues unabated. It can be seen in the tourists who hunt for 10 Rillington Place or who have their pictures taken in front of Marc Dutroux's seven houses. Madame Tussaud's chamber still exists, although it has expanded to become more gruesome than ever, and wax museums bearing her name have spread around the world.

Many other chambers of horror have been built since the time of Madame Tussaud, but some of them have not been restricted to the display of waxworks. In 1983, for example, serial killers

Charles Ng and Leonard Lake constructed a special chamber within a concrete bunker, in which they tortured, raped and killed an untold number of women. Austrian electronics engineer Josef Fritzl was no less heartless and calculating when he held his daughter prisoner in a series of specially-built subterranean chambers. She remained there for 24 years while her father sexually abused her on a daily basis. Some of the children she bore were also imprisoned.

Depraved as these men were, their actions are overshadowed by the sheer scale of the crimes that were committed by H. H. Holmes, the medical doctor who built over one hundred windowless rooms in a vast Chicago 'castle'. Within their soundproofed walls he tortured, mutilated, raped and murdered his many unsuspecting victims.

A lot of the monsters in this book did not go as far as building special chambers in which to perpetrate their ghastly crimes: their violent acts were committed in everyday rooms within their own unassuming houses. Fred West and his wife Rosemary dedicated a specific area of their home to their activities, while David Parker Ray set aside several rooms in his rural New Mexico bungalow. Each of the rooms was fitted with a range of implements that matched a specific type of torture, but none of them were as well-equipped as the semi-trailer that was parked in his front garden.

Ray called the trailer his 'Toy Box', while Fred West referred to the cellar he had adapted for rape as 'the Torture Chamber', but most of these degenerates had no special names for the rooms in which they committed their crimes. More often than not, their chambers of horror were simply known as 'the bedroom', 'the kitchen' or, ironically, 'the living room'.

What happens to these houses and apartment buildings once their secrets are revealed? Abduction, torture and murder can have a very negative effect on property values, yet most of them are still standing. There are some exceptions. For example, the home of Anthony Sowell, where the remains of 11 of his victims were found, was demolished by the authorities. Its destruction was prompted by the memory of the truly horrific crimes that had taken place within its walls.

The house in which Fred and Rosemary West carried out their abominable crimes stood empty for years after its occupants had been taken away in handcuffs and their children had been removed. In 1997 it was sold at auction for a bargain price and three years later it was sold for a second time. The buyer planned on renting it out, but with no takers the three-storey house was eventually demolished. A very attractive walkway has been built in its place.

The rubble from 25 Cromwell Street was taken away and pulverized at a secret location, far from the public gaze, because it was thought that the fragments would have attracted the wrong sort of attention. During its years of notoriety the house had been the target of souvenir-seeking vandals, who had taken pieces of the property as mementoes.

Number 10 Rillington Place – once the most notorious address in England, if not the world – stood for nearly two decades after its tenant, John Reginald Christie, was arrested. Once the bodies had been taken away and the investigation into the murders had been concluded, the house was again rented out. The address gained a whole new set of tenants, who seemingly had no qualms about using a kitchen that had once contained three putrefying bodies. In 1970, a film, *10 Rillington Place*, was made about Christie's crimes, but the tenants refused to vacate the premises so the film crew had to use Number 7 instead. The scene of Christie's infamous activities was demolished in the following year, but that was only because it was part of a massive redevelopment project. Camera crews were swiftly dispatched to film its destruction.

John Marlowe
Montreal, Quebec, Canada

MICHAEL ALIG

Bathroom Bloodbath

At the corner of 20th Street and 6th Avenue in Manhattan stands an impressive Gothic Revival building. Designed by the respected 19th-century Anglo-American architect Richard Upjohn, it owes its existence to William Augustus Muhlenberg, a Protestant Episcopal clergyman.The building began its life as the Church of the Holy Communion – John Jacob Astor and Cornelius Vanderbilt were among its parishioners.

The Reverend Muhlenberg hoped that the building would provide 'an oasis of Christian activity in the city'.

There was certainly a lot of activity. For over one hundred years, the church played an important role in the advancement of women, minorities and the poor within the community. By 1976, however, its once large congregation had dwindled to such an extent that it merged with two neighbouring parishes. The deconsecrated building became a drug rehabilitation centre and then a nightclub

Party animal Michael Alig was a flamboyant gossip with a taste for celebrity

called the Limelight. Finally, in 1996, this former oasis of Christian activity became linked with one of New York's most talked-about murders.

The guilty party, Michael Alig, was born on 29 April 1966 in South Bend, Indiana. His mother, a German immigrant, had a certain flair that made her stand out in the modestly-sized Midwestern city. Her eccentrically decorated home was filled with faux European furniture, for instance. Michael was equally unconventional. He liked to wear women's clothing – something his mother encouraged – and he immersed himself in television shows like *Dark Shadows*. Despite the bullying he had to endure as a gay teenager, Michael was an outstanding student. A flamboyant gossip with a taste for celebrity, he did not attempt to hide his sexuality.

Avant-garde creatures

With a population of roughly 300,000, South Bend was Indiana's fourth-largest city, but it was too small for Michael. After graduating from high school, Michael left for New York City, where he attended Fordham University. He did not graduate, but then he did not graduate from his next school either. By 1983, New York's club scene had brought his studies to a halt.

Michael did not just want to be a part of New York's nightlife – he wanted to be one of its guiding lights. He started by sweeping floors, bussing tables and running errands for Danceteria and the Palladium, the two most prominent clubs in 1980s New York. While he was doing this he came into contact with a number of avant-garde creatures of the night such as Ernie Glam, Richie Rich, Kenny Kenny, the beautiful transexual Amanda Lepore and James St James. Michael often showed up wearing trousers that had been cut away to expose his buttocks. He was brilliant at attracting attention to himself. Each year he held a Filthy Mouth Contest at which participants would try to outdo one another in screaming obscenities. He also led lightning-strike parties. Participants would suddenly descend on a McDonald's or a subway station, where they would hold illegal parties. Alig and his followers became known as the Club Kids.

Village Voice gossip columnist, Michael Musto, who saw these things and much more, once described Alig and the Club Kids as 'terminally superficial' with 'dubious aesthetic values'. They were 'master manipulators, exploiters, and, thank God, partiers'. He compared them to the Manson Family. The Club Kids were a perfect fit for *Geraldo*, *The Joan Rivers Show* and other voyeuristic talk shows.

'I think you want to have a good time in life and not hurt anybody,' said Joan at the end of their first television appearance.

The Club Kids were paid to be seen. They were living accessories.

Michael's highest point came with Disco 2000, a hedonistic event that he held every Wednesday at the Limelight. It was an evening fuelled by a mix of alcohol and drugs, which had the 'Unnatural Acts Review' as its focal point. No one quite knew what to expect. Spectators were able to witness a range of bizarre acts, from a man drinking his own urine to a woman rubbing herself against an amputee's stump. All of this happened within the walls of what had once been the Church of the Holy Communion.

An 'Emergency Room' was set up, in which 'doctors' and 'nurses' would prescribe ecstasy, ketamine and marijuana to their 'patients'. Prescriptions were filled by attendant dealers.

The blatant presence of drugs would have surprised no one – it was right there in Michael's flyers. The Club Kids had even talked about drug use on *The Phil Donahue Show*.

One of the people selling drugs at the Limelight and other Club Kids venues was twenty-something Andre Melendez. The son of Colombian immigrants, this former male prostitute turned up shortly after the Club Kids' appearance on *The Joan*

Club Kids and other denizens of the Limelight:
(from the left) Alig, Richie Rich and Nina Hagen, plus others

15

Rivers Show. His standard white outfit included aviator goggles, a white cap and wings, which made him particularly easy to spot in dark nightclubs lit by black lights.

Andre – or 'Angel', as he fancied himself – never quite fitted in with the other Club Kids. Alig's close friend James St James declared that the drug dealer strutted around the former Church of the Holy Communion as if he were 'God's Own Cousin'. And then there were the ridiculous wings, those dingy old wings, 'always knocking off my wig or spilling my drink. Oh, he was such a nightmare!' Another thing that rubbed James up the wrong way was the fact that Angel was every bit the businessman. Where other dealers were perfectly happy to cut the Club Kids some slack, sometimes filling 'prescriptions' for free, Angel was a stickler for being paid.

As the Limelight's notoriety grew, it became the target of repeated raids by the authorities. Angel was now a liability. Tossed out and forbidden to return, he would sometimes rely on Michael for a place to sleep. It was not that the head of the Club Kids was being generous – it was just that he appreciated the convenience of having a supply of drugs close at hand. On more than one occasion, when Angel was out, Michael and his room-mate Robert 'Freeze' Riggs skimmed the dealer's drugs and cash without ever saying a word. At other times, Michael failed to pay for his drugs.

Savage attack

By the morning of 17 March 1996, which was a Sunday, the drug dealer could no longer contain his annoyance. Unfortunately, his visit to collect from Michael did not come at the best time. Michael's expensive Riverbank West apartment in no way reflected his financial status. The rent was paid by his employer Peter Gatien, the owner of the Limelight. Michael Alig spent every cent he ever got his hands on, so he had no money.

Standing in his bedroom, Michael denied that he owed Angel so much as a cent. After all, he had allowed the dealer to stay in his apartment rent free. Angel went over the top at that point. He attacked Michael vehemently, destroying a glass cabinet in the process. Freeze had been asleep in his own bedroom, but the commotion jolted him awake. After grabbing a hammer he rushed to help Michael. He then hit Angel on the head, but the blow only made Angel even angrier. When the dealer made a lunge for the hammer, Freeze struck him again. Angel then turned his attention back to Michael, which is when Freeze hit him for a third time. At this point he collapsed.

Michael and Freeze failed to agree about what happened next. Freeze claimed that Michael began choking the unconscious Angel, before putting a pillowcase over his head. The autopsy report indicated that the dealer had indeed died of asphyxiation, not the hammer blows to the head. Michael admitted that they then stole some drugs from the lifeless Angel, which they ingested before relaxing for a few hours. When the effects began to wear off, the pair tried to revive Angel, even going so far as to immerse him in a tub of cold water, but they noticed no air bubbles when they held his head under the surface.

Convinced that Angel was dead, Michael began pouring drain cleaner into his mouth, thinking that it would work as an embalming fluid. With Freeze's assistance he then sealed the dead man's mouth with duct tape, so that the liquid would not escape.

The pair did not know what to do next, so they took the

rest of Angel's drugs. After that they spent countless days in a narcotic haze – Freeze put the number at 'five to seven' – during which they held parties in their Riverbank West apartment. Killing Angel had solved so many problems. Not only had Michael erased his debt but he now had the money that Angel had been carrying on the day he died. With this considerable sum he was able to decorate what had been a sparsely furnished flat.

Michael's partying guests luxuriated in rooms that combined the baroque with the neo-classical. The only reminder of the apartment's grimy past came in the form of the growing stench that emanated from one of the bathrooms. One partygoer happened to see Angel's stiff arm dangling from the bathtub, but he assumed that a guest had passed out. No one even faintly suspected that Michael's new-found wealth had resulted from a homicide.

After a while, Michael began telling his friends about the murder. How could he not? Michael liked to talk, he liked to gossip, he liked to shock and most of all he liked being the centre of attention. The people he told did not know what to think. James St James believed Michael, while others thought he was trying to spread a rumour as part of an elaborate publicity stunt. Independently of Michael, another rumour was in circulation.

It was being whispered that Michael was planning a 'Welcome Back, Angel' theme party.

If any such party was being planned, it could not have been held in Michael and Freeze's flat. After two weeks of lying in the tub, Angel's body was giving off a nearly unbearable odour. Something had to be done so Freeze was sent off to Macy's, where he purchased two top-of-the-range chef's knives and a cleaver. After he returned, Michael swallowed several bags of heroin and then set to work on Angel. He hacked off Angel's legs and then he wrapped them in plastic and placed them in duffle bags. Freeze tossed them into the Hudson River. For some unexplained reason, Michael also cut off Angel's genitals – what happened to them is unknown. What remained of Angel was put into a large garbage bag. This in turn was placed in a box that had contained the television that Michael had bought with the dealer's money. Freeze threw in some baking soda, hoping that it might absorb some of the foul odour.

At that point, the pair's judgement seemed to be clouded by drugs. Making no attempt at secrecy, they borrowed a trolley from the doorman and then took the box down in the main lift. When the lift doors opened, they calmly crossed the lobby and called a taxi. After securing the box in his cab's open boot, the driver drove the pair and their heavy package to the Hudson. Michael and Freeze watched the vehicle fade from view before pushing the box and its contents into the river. They were surprised when it floated rather than sank. Some packaging material had been left in the box, which had perhaps made it more buoyant.

Michael and Freeze might have got away with it if Michael had kept his mouth shut, but the accusations were now beginning to swirl around him. He could not have been surprised when in April 1996 Michael Musto, the columnist who had documented so many of his antics, ran a blind item in *The Village Voice*. It described how 'Mr. Mess' and 'Mr. Dealer' were fighting over money when in walked 'Mr. Mess #2', who hit 'Mr. Dealer' with a hammer. The five-sentence piece, a remarkably accurate summary of what had taken place in the Riverbank West apartment in the previous month, was picked up by another *Voice* reporter, Frank Owen. A few issues later, the newspaper published a front-page story about the murder.

Lost sparkle

By this time, the suspect was on the run. Michael sold all of the furniture he had bought just days before, borrowed $1,600 from Gatien and headed west with his friend Gitsie. When the drugs Michael had bought for the journey ran out in Colorado, he turned around and made for his mother's house. In June, Michael was drawn back to New York, where he again sought the world's attention.

He attempted to kick-start his career by hosting a party – but the sequins had lost their glitter. The rumours about Angel's demise hung over him like a cloud, so he found himself ostracized by the party crowd. Some people did show up, but a significant percentage of them were plain-clothes detectives and reporters chasing a murder story.

Meanwhile, the old television box containing Angel's torso, head and arms had been found washed up on the shore of the Hudson River. After being wrongly identified as those of an Asian male, the remains lay in the morgue for months. However, in November the error was realized and corrected. It soon became clear to the police that the stories that circulated around Michael were not just the outpourings of a publicity-seeking promoter. They managed to locate Freeze and three hours later they had a full written confession.

Michael had been harder to find, but he was finally picked up when they noticed his name and address on the bulletin board of a friend.

The party's over

The case against Michael was hard to mount because there had been another person in the apartment on the morning of the murder, apart from Freeze and Angel. Daniel Auster, the heroin addict son of novelist Paul Auster, had been sleeping in Freeze's bedroom when Angel arrived. Auster told several contradictory stories, none of which quite fitted in with Freeze's confession.

Another inconvenience for the prosecution was the presence of Michael's blood. While he had done his best to clean up after his struggle with Angel, there was evidence that he had received significant injuries when he had been slammed into the glass cabinet, which served to support the possibility of self-defence. Michael and Freeze accepted identical deals: ten to twenty years' imprisonment in exchange for a plea of manslaughter in the first degree.

There were several Club Kids in attendance when Michael and Freeze had their day in court on 1 October 1997, but the Alig, Riggs and Melendez families were not represented. No members of Michael's family attended his sentencing.

Freeze read from a long speech, in which he expressed great regret for his actions, but Michael had prepared nothing.

'I came here today not prepared to accept my sentence,' he began. 'So I didn't come with a speech because I was told we were going to postpone for another week, two weeks, or something like that, I don't know.'

Michael went on to claim that he had only agreed to his plea after being lied to and intimidated. 'And I feel terrible that I have nothing to say,' he concluded.

The judge, Justice William Wetzel, would have none of it. 'You are the victim?' he asked.

'In a way.'

'I don't think you are the victim. I think that Angel Melendez is the victim. He is the victim of your selfish, uncontrolled ego that has yet to be harnessed, that has yet to face reality. For you, the show is over. The party is over.'

The party might have ended, but Michael Alig's celebrity continues. Less than a year into his sentence, he was the subject of a documentary – *Party Monster: The Shockumentary*. In 2003, his story was turned into a feature film starring Macaulay Culkin, which was also called *Party Monster*. James St James then wrote a very entertaining book, *Disco Bloodbath*, about the Angel Melendez murder. He also made a habit of recording his telephone conversations with Michael. Some of them have been included in his regular Internet blog.

Twice denied parole, the former Club Kid has not exactly been a model prisoner. Heroin and Percocet (a narcotic pain reliever) have been found in his system. Even a prison sentence cannot save Michael Alig from himself.

ROBERT BERDELLA
A Room for his Sex Toys

obert ('Bob') Berdella told everybody about his time at the Kansas City Art Institute. It had been back in 1967, just as the Summer of Love was ending. He was 18 then, a young gay man who was away from his Ohio home for the first time. Berdella enjoyed his time at KCAI – he'd always been a good student – and he hoped that he would one day join the faculty as a professor. But he was to be disappointed. Although he had a significant talent it never quite matched up to his aspirations, so he became a chef. It was not the best-paying job, so he supplemented his income by dealing in drugs on the side. He was twice arrested for possession, but he escaped a jail sentence on each occasion.

Berdella never left Kansas City. Indeed, he put down roots by purchasing a house at 4315 Charlotte Street. It was quite large for an unattached gay man living alone, but Berdella fancied himself as something of a collector. Books, art and anything else

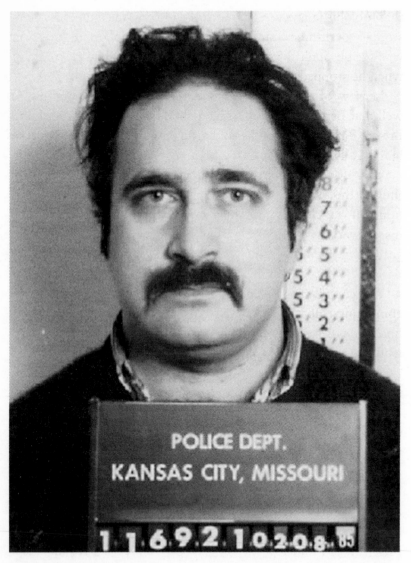

POLICE DEPT.
KANSAS CITY, MISSOURI

1 1 6 9 2 1 0 2 0 8 85

Berdella's master bedroom contained two skulls and envelopes full of teeth

that took his fancy were gathered up and crammed into his three-storey woodframe house. Most of what he collected, however, was simply junk. His house became increasingly cluttered and when he stopped cleaning up after his dogs it began to stink.

In view of the insanitary conditions at home, it was just as well that Berdella gave up being a chef. He opened a shop, Bob's Bizarre Bazaar, in which he sold drug paraphernalia, folk art, lava lamps and occult items.

The people on Charlotte Street saw him as a good neighbour, though they weren't too happy about the declining state of his house. It was clear that Berdella was not interested in maintaining his property. On the other hand, he appeared to be keen on gardening. He was always working in his back yard, often after dark.

Berdella always seemed ready to give something back to the community. He was an active participant in the local neighbourhood watch scheme and he was willing to open his doors to troubled young men who had nowhere to stay. These acts of charity attracted some unwanted attention in 1985, when police investigators contacted Berdella concerning two missing men.

The first of these was Jerry Howell, who was just 19 years old when he vanished on 5 July 1984. The other missing man was 25-year-old James Ferris, who had gone missing on 26 September 1985. Both men had been seen in Berdella's company. How did the investigators know this? They had been told by a third young man, Todd Stoops. Although Berdella admitted that he knew the two missing men, he denied being involved in their disappearances. The Kansas City police department kept Berdella under surveillance for a time, before moving on to other investigations.

Almost a year later, in June 1986, Todd Stoops disappeared too.

On the evening of 29 March 1988, Berdella was driving through a part of Kansas City that was known for male prostitutes when he spotted a good-looking 22-year-old named Chris Bryson.

It was all too easy to get the young, married man into his brown Toyota Tercel. All he needed to do was pass on an invitation to a 'party'. In fact, it seemed as if the party had already begun. As he drove to his Charlotte Street home, Berdella drank one beer after another.

Injected in the neck

Bryson was not put off by the smell or the junk inside Berdella's home, nor was he frightened of the overweight man who had picked him up. When Berdella suggested that they should go upstairs to get away from his three chow chow dogs, Bryson agreed. As Bryson reached the top landing, he was struck on the back of his head. Berdella then jabbed a hypodermic needle into his neck and he slumped down. Bryson had seconds to reconsider his host before losing consciousness.

Drugged and gagged

Berdella dragged his latest catch into the bedroom and stripped off his clothing. Over the next few hours he played around with the unconscious man, taking photographs all the while. Berdella was always careful to document his activities with his victims. When Bryson came round he found himself tied up in spread-eagle fashion, with a pillowcase over his head. When it was removed, the captive man knew from his blurred vision that he had been drugged. Roughly seven hours had passed since Berdella had knocked him out. Though he was gagged Bryson did his best to communicate, but his unintelligible pleas for mercy had the opposite effect on his captor.

Then Berdella began to torture the young man. For whatever sick reason, he concentrated his violence on Bryson's eyes, poking them with his fingers and applying an unknown liquid that caused a stinging sensation. He then sat on his sex slave, before hitting the young man's bound hands with an iron bar. Not content with that, he attached wires to Bryson's genitals and thighs and then ran an electric current through them. After a few more photographs, Berdella gave Bryson another two injections.

It was when the young man regained consciousness for a second time that his captor explained his situation to him. Bryson was told that he was now Berdella's sex toy and his punishments were designed to reinforce the fact. Should Bryson refuse to accept his new position in life, his suffering would only worsen. In fact, he might 'end up in the trash', like the others before him. Bryson did his best to follow Berdella's wishes but the torture continued, despite his subservience. He endured electric shocks and rape and at one point Berdella injected drain cleaner into his throat.

All the while, the captive man was looking for an opportunity to escape. But was escape possible? Berdella made a point of showing him pictures of his discarded sex toys: the men in the photographs appeared to be dead. Although little is known about what happened to Berdella's other captives, Chris Bryson's experiences are well documented.

The reason is quite simple: he lived to tell the world about his ordeal. On 4 April 1988, five days into Bryson's nightmare,

Berdella made a mistake that would ultimately cost him his freedom. Before leaving 4315 Charlotte Street that day he made certain to tie Bryson up as usual. But this time he altered his routine by binding his victim's hands in front of him, instead of tying them to the bed. Fortunately, Bryson was clear-headed enough to pick up some matches, light them and then methodically burn through the ropes that secured his wrists.

When he had managed to free himself, Bryson rushed for the open window and jumped through it. He fell two storeys to the ground. Wearing nothing but a dog collar and a leash, he then started running. Terrified and disorientated, Bryson acted very much like an escaped animal. He sprinted through Berdella's neighbourhood without seeking help. It was obvious that he had no destination in mind. He just wanted to run and keep running.

Bryson's headlong progress was halted when he was cornered by two police cars. After noting the collar and leash, the officers in attendance thought he had been a willing participant in a sex game that had gone wrong. At first, Bryson could not tell them otherwise because the mental and physical torture had rendered him barely capable of speech. Eventually, he was able to identify himself and communicate just some of the horrors he had endured.

Bryson was in the hospital when Berdella returned home, but by then the police had a good description of him – and they had his address. The overweight 39-year-old was arrested outside his home on a charge of sexual assault. Defiant to the end, he did not allow the investigators to enter his Charlotte Street house, so they were forced to wait for a search warrant. There was one other obstacle: Berdella's chow chows. When the warrant came through, the police officers were accompanied by animal control specialists.

Incriminating photographs

After the dogs had been led away, the detectives moved to the second floor where they discovered the room in which Bryson had been held. Its contents were much as the victimized man had described. They found the burned rope, the syringes and the sinister electrical device that had been used to administer shocks. Moving to the next room, the investigators found a box of photographs. Some were of Bryson, but the remainder featured other victims. All of the men had been bound and gagged and they were obviously in distress.

Even so, the police officers still entertained the suspicion that Berdella's victims had been his willing lovers. Any such thoughts quickly vanished when they entered the third upstairs room, which was the master bedroom. It contained two skulls, two envelopes full of teeth and Berdella's detailed records of the torture he had meted out to each victim. The more the authorities looked, the more they turned up. In one bedroom closet they discovered a bag filled with human vertebrae. There was also a wallet that had belonged to a man who had been reported missing.

Berdella was arraigned on the day of his arrest. The first charges against him were confined to the offences that he had committed against Chris Bryson. There was one count of felonious restraint and another of first degree assault, followed by seven counts of sodomy. By this time, however, the investigators were sure that the shop owner had committed far more serious crimes in the past.

A mechanical digger was taken to the yard in which Berdella

had done his night-time gardening. The machine's shovel only had to enter the soft earth twice before it came up with a human skull.

The investigation was not limited to Berdella's house. Detectives combed the streets worked by male prostitutes, looking for anyone

The authorities dug deep: the skull in the garden belonged to 20-year-old Larry Pearson

who would talk. They soon discovered that Berdella had something of a reputation. In fact, he was considered to be dangerous. After shuffling through hundreds of photographs Berdella had taken, the police officers identified roughly twenty men. However, it was nearly impossible to establish just how many people had been murdered by the former chef.

Meanwhile, the forensic examiners were beginning to come up with some names. One of the skulls in Berdella's bedroom was found to belong to Robert Sheldon, an 18-year-old who had disappeared in April 1985. The skull that had been dug up in Berdella's garden belonged to 20-year-old Larry Pearson, who had been missing since 9 July 1987.

Armed with Berdella's photographs, and a 58-page journal in which he had detailed his crimes, the prosecutors began to lay further charges against the degenerate sex offender. As they did so, the suspect surprised both the police and the prosecutors by offering a full confession in exchange for a life sentence. With the threat of the death penalty out of the way he had nothing to lose. On 13 December 1988 he began the first of what would be three days of testimony.

Berdella told the hearing that his first victim had been Jerry Howell, whose disappearance had been investigated three years earlier. The murderer said that his physical relationship with Howell had soured when he had refused to pay back money he owed. In retaliation, Berdella tortured Howell before finally killing him. The next thing was to dispose of the corpse. Before he dismembered the body, he hung it upside down so the blood would drain from it. The sight excited him so much that he felt the need to take photographs. Eventually he cut the corpse up, using kitchen knives and a chainsaw. He then placed the pieces into a number of plastic bags, in time for the weekly refuse collection.

Berdella's second victim was Robert Sheldon, an 18-year-old who had stayed at the Charlotte Street house on several occasions. Sheldon's ordeal began on 19 April 1985, when he was subjected to a torture regime that was similar to that which had been meted out to Howell. Berdella admitted that he had intended to keep the teenager for a significant length of time. To this end, he injected Drano (a drain-cleaning product) into Sheldon's left eyeball, thinking that blindness would make the young man even more subservient. And yet Berdella killed Sheldon after only four days because he feared that his captive might be discovered by another visitor.

Berdella disposed of the teenager's body by cutting it up in his bath. He put the remains out with the rubbish – except for the head, which he buried in his garden.

The murderer's experiments with electrocution began two months later when he claimed his third victim, Mark Wallace. After only a few days, the 20-year-old man was killed, dismembered and put out on the kerb for collection by the dustmen.

Terrible deaths

Berdella's fourth victim, Walter Ferris, signed his own death warrant in September 1985 when he made the mistake of asking the shop owner whether he could stay at his house for a while. Berdella claimed that his death was an accident, the result of a lethal combination of drugs, and yet there was evidence of torture.

Todd Stoops, the young man who had informed the police

about Berdella, was the next person to die. He had been advised to keep his distance from the suspect, but he had not listened. Berdella took Stoops captive on 17 June 1986 and he died two weeks later, perhaps because of the injuries he suffered when Berdella pushed his fist up the young man's rectum.

More than a year passed before Berdella killed again. Larry Pearson, a 20-year-old male prostitute, was the last victim to die. More submissive than the others, he became Berdella's sex toy for about six weeks. Then quite unexpectedly he began to fight back, so he was killed.

On 19 December 1988 Berdella appeared in court. He pleaded guilty to one count of first-degree murder and four counts of second-degree murder. Having fulfilled his part of the deal with the state he would be spared the death penalty.

Although Bob Berdella would spend the rest of his life in prison, his sentence would be a short one. Less than four years later, on 8 October 1992, he died of a heart attack.

PAUL BERNARDO AND KARLA HOMOLKA
Murder in the Love Shack

aul Bernardo's life began with an act of betrayal. Kenneth Bernardo, an accountant, married Marilyn, Paul's mother, in 1960. They settled in Scarborough, a suburb that has since been swallowed up by the City of Toronto, and within three years they were the proud parents of a son and a daughter. However, theirs was not a happy marriage for Kenneth was allegedly abusive towards his wife. Paul was conceived when Marilyn sought comfort in the arms of an old boyfriend, so he was not Kenneth's son.

Kenneth knew the truth but he had no issue with the baby being given his name. However, Paul Kenneth Bernardo's birth on 27 August 1964 did nothing to improve the couple's deteriorating relationship. Kenneth took to walking around the neighbourhood at night, peeping through windows. He then appeared in court, accused of fondling a young girl. Worst of all, the accountant began sexually abusing his own daughter.

Unlike Kenneth, Marilyn rarely ventured outside the home. She became increasingly reclusive, eventually seeking solitude in the basement. Yet despite the unhealthy atmosphere that prevailed in the Bernardo home, Paul appeared to be a healthy and happy boy. It was almost as if he was blissfully ignorant of his mother's massive weight gain, her depression and her eccentric behaviour. Whether Paul knew anything of Kenneth's abusive behaviour or his brushes with the law is a mystery.

Paul's teachers saw him as gifted and hardworking and his after-school employers found him to be diligent and dependable. And no girl would turn down the opportunity to go out on a date with Paul Bernardo. The future looked very bright indeed for the blond boy from Scarborough.

Personality change

Then, at the age of 16, Paul's world was turned upside down. What had begun as a simple argument between mother and son changed into something else altogether when Marilyn presented Paul with a photograph of a man he had never seen. So it was that the teenager learned that Kenneth was not his biological father. This was how he learned that his mother had been unfaithful and that he was a bastard. Paul never forgave his mother. From that point onwards he would refer to her as a 'whore'. His attitude towards other women, perhaps all women, underwent a radical change.

Suddenly, Paul was no longer the boy that the high school

girls had found so considerate and caring. He started going out to bars, where he picked up women by telling lies about who he was and what he had accomplished.

In the process, he developed a preference for anal sex and bondage, often beating his girlfriends into submission.

Paul's altered personality did not only manifest itself in his treatment of women. While studying at the University of Toronto, the former Boy Scout began an illegal business smuggling cigarettes from the United States into Canada. Nineteen-eighty-seven proved to be a momentous year for Paul. He graduated from university, accepted a job as a junior accountant at Price Waterhouse and met a woman who was in so very many respects his soul mate.

Her name was Karla Homolka and she was unlike any woman he had ever known. The feisty 17-year-old enjoyed being bound and she wanted to be dominated. The couple's romance progressed at a rapid pace. Barely two months elapsed between their first meeting in a Scarborough restaurant and their engagement. The couple's Boxing Day engagement celebration might have been big news to the Bernardos and the Homolkas, but Paul was receiving even greater attention from the public at large. Although no one knew his true identity, he had become known as the 'Scarborough Rapist'.

Paul's method was remarkably consistent. He would overpower his victims just after they had disembarked from a bus and then he would force them to have anal and oral sex. It is believed that he sexually assaulted a total of 13 women between May 1987 and July 1990, much to Karla's delight. One victim reported that a young woman had been videotaping her assault.

Over the years, Paul and Karla amassed quite a collection of tapes, all of which recorded their sexual exploits. A number of the recordings just featured the two of them, while others included women they had picked up in bars. Some of the sexual activities were consensual but many were not, particularly when Paul was carrying out his Scarborough Rapist attacks.

The incident involving Karla's 15-year-old sister Tammy was perhaps even more shocking than Paul's attacks on strangers. Tammy's virginity was Karla's Christmas gift to Paul, though it was hardly a surprise. In fact, the whole idea had originated with the young accountant. Paul had found it hard to accept the fact that Karla was not a virgin when they had met, but he felt that taking her sister's virginity would set things right.

Karla thought that her job as a veterinary assistant would help with the rape. Dogs and other animals were regularly given sedatives at her place of work, which gave her access to all sorts of medication. She decided to go with Halcion, a regular sedative, and Halothane, an anaesthetic inhalant that is used in veterinary surgery.

On 23 December 1990 Paul and Karla served Tammy alcoholic drinks laced with Halcion in the basement of the Homolka home. They videotaped the girl's descent into unconsciousness and then they waited. When the rest of the house – Karla's parents and her other sister Lori – had gone to bed, Tammy was stripped naked. As Karla held a Halothane-soaked rag over Tammy's face Paul turned the video camera back on and raped her. When Karla's fiancé had finished it was her turn to sexually assault Tammy.

It was just the sort of Christmas gift that Paul had wanted. He had taken Tammy's virginity and he was enjoying watching the sight of his future bride molesting her unconscious sister.

Then Tammy vomited.

Relying on her very limited veterinary knowledge, Karla

held her sister upside down in an effort to clear her air passage, but the unconscious girl was choking. Within minutes she was dead. Paul and Karla called 911, but not until they had wasted precious minutes dressing Tammy. They also had to find a good hiding place for the video camera and the stolen drugs. Fast asleep in their beds, the rest of the household knew nothing of the drama taking place below. In fact, the Homolka parents did not know anything was amiss until an ambulance drew up in front of their house.

For such an intelligent young man, Paul was taking all sorts of unnecessary risks. He always spoke to his victims and many saw the white Ford Capri that he drove. What is more, Paul never made any attempt to hide his face. In December 1987 a composite drawing of the rapist looked so much like Paul that the police received calls from his acquaintances, his fellow employees at Price Waterhouse and the bank at which he had his account. When he was visited by two police detectives he agreed to provide blood, saliva and hair samples and in April 1992 he was one of five suspects who had not been ruled out by the police. But at that point the hunt for the Scarborough Rapist was no longer a priority. It seemed that he had ended his attacks.

Sexual assaults

Paul was still raping girls and young women, however. It was just that these crimes were now taking place in the city of St Catharines, on the opposite shore of Lake Ontario. It was in this rather attractive city that the betrothed couple set up house in February 1991. Their home was a rented two-storey wood frame construction at number 57 Bayview Drive. It may not have been the mansion of Paul's dreams, but it was a start – and it was a mere 30 km (18 miles) from the United States border, so it was perfect for his cigarette smuggling business.

What is more, it was a place in which he was able to carry out his more elaborate sexual assaults in privacy.

Paul's first rape victim at 57 Bayview Drive was a girl who is known only as 'Jane Doe'. A 15-year-old friend of Karla's – someone who bore a striking resemblance to Tammy – she had accepted an invitation to visit the couple's new home. During the evening, Jane was given alcoholic drinks laced with the sedative Halcion. She quickly passed out.

Karla had given Tammy to Paul as a Christmas gift and now she was giving Jane Doe to him. She was a present from a bride to her future husband. Until the girl was given to him, Paul knew nothing of Karla's plans.

The unconscious girl was undressed, the video camera came out and Paul began filming. Both of them had sex with Jane.

Paul took her virginity and raped her anally.

When Jane woke up the next morning she was sore and sick to her stomach – but she was entirely unaware of the horrors she had suffered. Karla then introduced her friend to Paul. She did not recognize him, which made it clear that she did not recall the events of the previous evening.

Locked out

The couple's next victim was a 14-year-old girl named Leslie Mahaffy. After arriving home in the early hours of 15 June 1991, Leslie found herself locked out. She was spotted by Paul, who forced her at knifepoint into his car and drove to the home he shared with his sleeping fiancée. Karla awoke to the sight of a naked, blindfolded girl who was being videotaped by her future husband. Following Paul's directions, Karla sexually assaulted Leslie before taking hold of the video camera herself. She then filmed Paul as he tortured and raped the girl.

Later that morning, Leslie was killed. Exactly what happened is a mystery. Karla claimed that Paul strangled Leslie, while Paul maintained that Karla fed the girl a lethal dose of Halcion. The cause of death was difficult to determine because Paul cut up Leslie's corpse before encasing her remains in concrete blocks.

Before he did so, Karla helped him to move the dead girl's body to the basement. They had some entertaining to do because it was Father's Day. Karla's parents and her sister Lori would eat a celebratory dinner unaware of the dead body that lay beneath them.

At some point, Paul and Karla transported the cement blocks containing Leslie's body to Lake Gibson, just 10 km (6 miles) from Bayview Drive. But Paul had once again exposed himself to risk. He had disposed of the cement blocks in relatively shallow water, when the lake was much deeper elsewhere. The blocks were discovered on 29 June 1991 – Paul and Karla's wedding day.

What happened next is unclear. It is known that Karla and Paul again assaulted Jane Doe in August. There was almost certainly another victim – but is it possible that there was more than one? What can be said with certainty is that the pair were responsible for the murder of 15-year-old Kristen French, who was abducted on 16 April 1992. Karla lured the girl to the couple's gold Nissan 240SX by pretending to be lost. As the teenager stood looking at a map, Paul put a knife to her throat and forced her into the back seat. All of this took place in a church car park.

Kristen was then taken to the young couple's home, where she was sexually abused and tortured. After three days, she was killed. The couple's stories contradicted each other when they were finally brought to justice, but according to Karla Paul began beating the girl with a rubber mallet as she tried to escape. He then strangled her with an electrical cord.

Two weeks after she disappeared her dead body was found in a ditch just a short walk from the place where Leslie's severed remains had been laid to rest.

This second killing rocked St Catharines, a city with a population of only 130,000 inhabitants. It had suffered the murder of two teenage girls in less than a year.

A special Green Ribbon Task Force was formed, a hotline was set up and the tips began to flow.

Paul's name again came to the surface, just as it had during the hunt for the Scarborough Rapist. But when the police visited his Bayview Drive home there was no trace of the horrors that had taken place within its walls only weeks earlier. The Bernardo home was found to be clean and orderly – more so, perhaps, than those of most couples in their early twenties. During his interview with police, Paul seemed to be both respectful and respectable. The detectives never interviewed Karla.

However, the net began to close in February 1993, when a second analysis of the blood samples from the Scarborough Rapist investigation showed that Paul was guilty of at least three of the assaults. Two years had passed since the blood had been collected. During that time, two girls had been sexually assaulted and murdered.

Detectives placed Paul under surveillance, but it was not what they saw that brought about his arrest.

The newlywed had begun beating his wife – and there was nothing sexual in the violence. Karla's black eyes and other bruises could not be ignored by her parents. On 5 January 1993 they persuaded their daughter to leave Paul. He was arrested the next day and was charged with assaulting his wife with a weapon. Karla was questioned for nearly five hours, during which it became all too apparent that the police were aware that Paul was the Scarborough Rapist and was also the murderer of Leslie Mahaffy and Kristen French.

Karla promptly hired a lawyer, a man whose dog she had cared for in her work as a veterinary assistant, and she watched in horror as Paul was arrested. When the police began searching the Bayview Drive house in the middle of February, Karla knew they would find incriminating evidence. Her lawyer managed to strike a deal with Ontario's attorney general. Karla would receive two concurrent 12-year sentences for her part in the murders of the teenage girls, in exchange for her testimony against Paul.

Willing accomplice

Murray Segal, who acted on behalf of the government during negotiations, seemed to have anticipated a public outcry over the agreement.

'Why not a greater penalty in light of the horrendous facts?' he said. 'Without her, the true state of affairs might never be known. A guilty plea is the traditional hallmark of remorse. Her age, her lack of criminal record, the abuse and the influence of her husband and her somewhat secondary role were factors. She's unlikely to re-offend.'

What he did not know was that Karla's participation in the murders of the two girls was much greater than she had led the world to believe. There was very clear and damning evidence to this effect – it was sitting there at 57 Bayview Drive and yet the police had missed it.

The videotapes that Paul and Karla had taken of their crimes against the girls were hidden in a hollow bathroom ceiling. They could be easily accessed by simply removing the light fixture.

When the tapes were played during Paul's trial in May 1995 they revealed that Karla had eagerly participated in the couple's sexual assaults on the two girls. It became obvious that her story about being manipulated by her husband was completely false. Particularly damning was the revelation that Kristen had been murdered so that the couple could enjoy an Easter dinner at the home of Karla's parents.

On 1 September 1995, Paul Bernardo was found guilty of a number of offences, including kidnapping, forcible confinement, aggravated sexual assault and first-degree murder. He was also found guilty of offering an indignity to Leslie Mahaffy's body.

Although he is eligible for parole in 2020, it is unlikely that he will ever be released.

Karla served her full 12-year sentence and she was released on 4 July 2005. It is uncertain where she is living, though one 2007 television report placed her in the Caribbean.

The house that Paul and Karla referred to as the 'Love Shack' was razed to the ground.

A new house, with a new civic address, now stands on the site where Leslie Mahaffy and Kristen French were so callously murdered.

PHILLIP GARRIDO
Backyard of the Baby Boomer

A baby boomer born within sight of San Francisco, Phillip Garrido was convinced that fame lay in his future. As a young man, he believed that he was destined for stardom as a rock musician. As the years passed, the dream faded and was replaced by the idea of becoming a messianic figure. In the end, he did achieve fame of a kind. However, only one person would ever look up to Phillip Garrido: his second wife, the woman who had helped him carry out his despicable crimes.

Phillip Craig Garrido entered the world on 5 April 1951 in Contra Costa County. His father Manuel, a fork lift operator, provided a modest, yet comfortable home. Little is known about Garrido's childhood, in part due to the fact that his father demanded money in exchange for information about his son.

That said, Garrido's early years may be inconsequential. It may just be that they weren't formative in creating the monster who would become fodder for television newscasts. No, according to some who knew Garrido, his anti-social, dangerous behaviour first began with a motorcycle accident he'd suffered as a teenager. On this, even his father was willing to share an opinion. According to Manuel, before the tragic event, Garrido had been a 'good boy'. And after? Well, he became uncontrollable and started to take drugs.

Despite his wild behaviour, Garrido graduated from local Liberty High School with the rest of his class. The year was

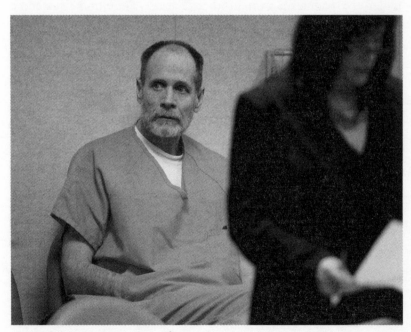

Garrido believed he had a special machine through which he communicated with God

1969, a time when American counterculture was pervasive. Garrido appeared to embrace it all. He grew his hair, bought a fringed leather jacket, and played bass in a psychedelic rock group. But in reality, the young high school graduate wanted little to do with peace and love. Eighteen years old, Garrido had already committed his first act of rape, and would regularly beat his girlfriend, Christine Perreira.

In 1972, he was charged with the rape of a 14-year-old girl whom he had plied with barbiturates. Garrido avoided doing time in prison when the girl refused to testify. What the authorities did not realize at the time was that they might have nailed the young man on another charge – Garrido had become one of the busiest drug dealers in Contra Costa County.

Once clear of the rape charge, Garrido married Christine. The young couple settled 300 kilometres (185 miles) to the northeast in South Lake Tahoe. In the small city, drugs were no longer the Garridos' primary source of income. Christine got a job dealing cards at Harrah's Casino, while her husband pursued his dream of becoming a rock star.

Perverted plan

Three years passed, and vinyl glory still eluded Garrido. Each day was blanketed in a haze induced by a combination of marijuana, cocaine and LSD. He would spend hours masturbating while watching elementary school girls across the street, but the real object of his interest was a woman. Garrido had been following her for months during which he developed a very elaborate plan, which he set in motion by renting a warehouse in Reno, 100 kilometres (60 miles) to the south. He then fixed up the space to his taste, hanging rugs for soundproofing. A mattress was brought in, as were satin sheets, bottles of wine and an extensive collection of pornographic magazines.

When the trap was set, Garrido took four tabs of LSD and attacked the woman whom he'd been stalking for so long. However, in his drugged state, she managed to fight him off. Frustrated, Garrido drove to Harrah's, where he asked one of his wife's co-workers, Katie Calloway Hall, for a lift home.

Katie was not as lucky as the intended victim. She ended up being raped repeatedly in Garrido's Reno warehouse. After eight hours, Katie was rescued by a police officer whose eye had been drawn to the door, which was left ajar.

This time, Christine did not stand by Garrido. After her husband's arrest, she severed all ties. The divorce came through just as Garrido was beginning a 50-year prison sentence in Leavenworth, Kansas.

However, for Garrido, romance was still in the air. Behind bars he began corresponding with the niece of a fellow inmate, Nancy Bocanegra, four years his junior, In 1981, the two were married in a ceremony that was conducted by the prison chaplin. Garrido was not yet one tenth of the way through his sentence. When not enjoying conjugal visits with Nancy, he would study psychology and theology. Religion, it seemed, became the focus of his life. A Catholic by birth, he converted, becoming a Jehovah's Witness. Garrido's extreme devotion to the denomination was cited by the prison psychologist as an indication that he would commit no further crimes.

Garrido was granted parole in 1988. With Nancy, he returned to South Lake Tahoe, where they spent nearly three uneventful years.

On 10 June 1991, Garrido's prison psychologist would

A walkway leads to the home of Phillip Garrido where Jaycee
Dugard was imprisoned for 18 years

be proven wrong. That morning, a man named Carl Probyn watched in horror as his 11-year-old step-daughter was dragged into a grey sedan. He was not alone – several of the girl's friends had also witnessed the abduction – and yet no one was able to provide the licence plate number of the car that sped away.

The girl, Jaycee Dugard, soon found herself living in sheds, tents and under tarpaulins in the backyard of a house in Contra Costa County. The property belonged to Garrido's mother, who was then suffering from dementia. Eventually, the old woman would be shipped off to a chronic care hospital. Jaycee, of course, remained on the property, where she would be subjected to 18 years of sexual abuse at Garrido's hands.

She bore her captor two children, both daughters, born in

August of 1994 and November of 1997. Both would come to describe Jaycee as an older sister. It is unknown whether or not they knew the truth.

The girl's nightmare could have ended earlier. Garrido fell under the watchful eyes of his neighbours when it was discovered that he was a registered sex offender.

In 2006, one of the watchful called police to report that Garrido, a 'psychotic sex addict', had a woman and several children living under tents in his backyard. A sheriff's deputy dispatched to investigate interviewed Garrido on his front porch; he did not bother to look at the backyard, nor did he run a background check.

Two years later, police were again on Garrido's property, accompanied by fire-fighters who had been called in to put out a blaze.

Weird and frightening

The actions of law enforcement officers might be considered lazy or negligent, but they paled beside the ineptitude displayed by the California Department of Corrections and Rehabilitation. As a convicted sex offender, Garrido was visited regularly by department employees. All the visits, both scheduled and unscheduled, took place while Jaycee was in the backyard. In nearly two decades, not one single department agent would bother investigating Garrido's collection of tents, tarpaulins and sheds.

The authorities might not have thought Garrido was a suspicious character, but those who saw him on a daily basis found him weird and just a little frightening. Neighbourhood parents told their children to keep away from his house. He ran a print shop, Printing for Less, but his behaviour ensured that he had few repeat customers. Those who gave him business would often find themselves subjected to bizarre ramblings. Garrido, the self-proclaimed 'Man Who Spoke with his Mind', would rant about how he could control sound with his mind. Some customers were privileged enough to be shown a machine, through which the printer claimed he could communicate with God. Others might be treated to recordings of songs that Garrido had written about his attraction to underage girls.

Garrido kept a blog, titled 'Voices Revealed', through which he attempted to convince others of his special relationship with God. The outlet seemed to encourage further writing. In August of 2009, he walked into the San Francisco offices of the FBI to hand-deliver two weighty tomes he had written: 'The Origin of Schizophrenia Revealed' and 'Stepping into the Light'. The latter was a personal story in which Garrido detailed how it was that he had come to triumph over his violent sexual urges. Intent on helping others to do the same, he approached Lisa Campbell, a special events coordinator at the University of California, Berkeley, with the idea of a lecture. Garrido was not alone when he made his proposal. Both his daughters sat in on the meeting, listening as their father spoke about his deviant past and the rapes he had committed.

It was Campbell's report of the strange behaviour to Garrido's parole officer that at long last brought an end to Jaycee's nightmare.

Moment of truth

When confronted, on 26 August 2009, Garrido admitted to kidnapping Jaycee, adding that he was the father of her children. Both he and Nancy were taken into custody.

On 28 April 2011, Garrido pleaded guilty to Jaycee's kidnapping, as well as 13 counts of sexual assault. Sitting next to her husband, Nancy pleaded guilty to the kidnapping, and one charge of aiding and abetting a sexual assault. In court, both of the defendants' lawyers portrayed their respective clients as good souls. After 1997, the year in which they both found God, the couple had dedicated themselves to Jaycee and the children – or so the claim went.

Garrido hoped his confession would win Nancy a lighter sentence. Whether or not he was successful is a matter of debate. What is certain, however, is that Nancy's sentence was not nearly

Nancy Garrido pleaded guilty to kidnapping as well as aiding and abetting a sexual assault

as harsh as that of her husband. Where Garrido received a term amounting to 431 years, Nancy was sentenced to 36 years in prison. Should she live a long life, Nancy Garrido will be ninety when she leaves prison.

DAVID AND CATHERINE BIRNIE
Death and the Common-law Bedroom

They were dubbed the 'Moorhouse Murderers' after their home address 3 Moorhouse Street, Willagee, Australia. Serial killers, together they had strangled and bludgeoned. Four young women and one girl had died at their hands. David and Catherine Birnie were seen as monsters, were hated and threatened. Yet David was small and slight, not much bigger than his wife Catherine. At first glance, this ordinary-looking couple seemed incapable of harming anyone. But that initial impression was all that was needed to lure their victims into their trap.

David Birnie was born in Subiaco, a suburb of Perth, on 16

February 1951, which is where he spent his childhood. The Birnies were seen as a problem family by their neighbours and fellow parishioners at Wattle Grove Baptist Church. There was gossip about affairs, drinking and incest, and the authorities took the Birnie children away from their parents on more than one occasion.

David met Catherine, who was just three months his junior, when her family moved in next door. The two soon became a couple. Catherine was an unhappy girl with no real friends. She had never known her mother, who had died when she was an infant, and she rarely saw her father. Although she had been raised by her grandparents, she felt unwanted, so David provided the affection that had been lacking in her life.

Attempted rape

Never a good student, David left school at the age of 15, intending to become a jockey. He became an apprentice at a nearby race track, where he worked for trainer Eric Parnham. There are conflicting accounts of David's behaviour during this time. Parnham maintains that David was a good worker who never did anything wrong, while others claim that he often displayed cruelty towards the horses. Whatever the truth, there was no doubt about the fact that he attempted to rob and rape the elderly landlady of his boarding house. The assault brought his job with Parnham to an end, together with all of his dreams of becoming a jockey.

Fortunately for David his landlady did not report his crime to the police and yet he learned nothing from the experience. He began burgling people's homes, often accompanied by Catherine. On 11 June 1969 the pair appeared at the Perth Police Court, where they pleaded guilty to 11 charges of breaking, entering and stealing. Among the stolen goods were items of welding equipment, which they used in an attempt to break into the safe of a drive-in cinema.

David was jailed for nine months – his first prison sentence – while Catherine was placed on probation. The authorities dealt leniently with Catherine because of her condition. The 18-year-old girl was pregnant with another man's child. Three weeks later, the couple were brought before the Supreme Court, where they faced more charges of breaking, entering and stealing. After pleading guilty, David's sentence was increased by a further three years, while Catherine's probation was extended by a further four years.

After serving just one year in prison David managed to escape. During his brief period of freedom he committed 53 further offences. Most of them involved breaking, entering and stealing, but mixed in with his haul were 100 sticks of gelignite and 120 detonators. As before, Catherine had been a willing accomplice. There was nothing she would not do for David, she told the court.

This time the authorities were not so forgiving. Catherine received a six-month jail sentence and her baby was taken away by welfare workers. A further two and a half years were added to David's other sentences. It now looked as if he would be spending most of the 1970s in prison.

Fairy tale romance

With David firmly behind bars, Catherine reluctantly moved on with her life. She accepted a position as a live-in domestic for a family in Fremantle and she fell in love with one of their sons.

It was a fairy tale romance with an elaborate wedding on Catherine's 21st birthday. Catherine soon gave birth to a baby boy, Donny. Her happiness came to an abrupt end seven months later, when she watched in horror as the child was crushed to death by a car.

Although five more children followed, the marriage was not happy. Catherine's thoughts increasingly turned to David and in 1983 she began seeing her old boyfriend again. David was also experiencing an unhappy marriage. After two years of sometimes not so clandestine meetings, Catherine picked up the telephone and told her husband that she was never coming back. And she kept her word.

David and Catherine then divorced their respective spouses. The reunited couple never married, but Catherine took David's name.

David had been obsessed by sex in his adolescent years. Now in his early thirties, his early compulsions had returned to him in full force. It was a Birnie family failing. His brother James had gone to prison for assaulting his 6-year-old niece.

'She led me on,' was his defence.

While it does not appear that David was similarly attracted towards young girls, he did have some rather unconventional tastes.

He quickly found others who shared his interests. Soon, he was hosting group encounters at the couple's modest home. Catherine eagerly took part in these orgies.

The couple were always looking for new sexual experiences and by 1986 they began discussing the abduction and sexual assault of young women. David told Catherine that she would experience intense orgasms when she saw him raping another woman.

On 6 October 1986 they kidnapped a pretty 22-year-old psychology student named Mary Neilson. She first met David at his place of employment, a Myaree scrap yard, on the outskirts of Perth. Mary needed tyres for her car and David told her that he had just what she was looking for at his home. When Mary crossed the threshold at 3 Moorhouse Street, she was threatened with a knife before being gagged and chained to a bed. David raped the woman repeatedly while Catherine watched. She even asked him questions about the experience.

After David had tired of Mary, he took her to Gleneagles National Park, where he raped her one last time. He then used a nylon cord to strangle her. When the girl was dead, David made a point of stabbing her. He mistakenly believed that the body needed to be perforated in order to allow gases to escape as it decomposed. Mary was then buried in a shallow grave. Six days after Mary had gone missing, her car was discovered in a car park that was directly across the street from Perth Police Station. David had driven it there himself.

Their second victim, 15-year-old Susannah Candy, was abducted, raped and murdered on the same day, 20 October. Susannah had been walking along the highway when the couple had picked her up. Once in the car, she was bound and gagged at knifepoint.

Chained to a bed

Like Mary Neilson, Susannah was chained to a bed at the Birnie home and then raped. This time, however, Catherine joined in. When they had finished, the couple tried to strangle the girl, but she fought back and they found it hard to keep her down. During the struggle they managed to force sleeping pills down their victim's throat. When the medication took effect, David put a cord around Susannah's neck and then asked Catherine to prove her love for him by killing the girl.

Catherine had no problem with fulfilling David's request.

'I didn't feel a thing,' she said later. 'It was like I expected. I was prepared to follow him to the end of the earth and do anything to see that his desires were satisfied. She was a female. Females hurt and destroy males.'

David and Catherine buried Susannah in the national park, close to Mary's remains.

On the evening of 1 November, 12 days after the abduction and murder of Susannah Candy, the Birnies were on the prowl for another victim.

They spotted a woman standing by her car on the shoulder of Canning Highway. Noelene Patterson, a 31-year-old bar manager, had run out of fuel on her drive home from work. In need of a lift, she readily got into the Birnies' car.

The abduction of Noelene upset the dynamics at 3 Moorhouse Street. Taken by his captive's beauty, David kept putting off her murder. Catherine's feelings of insecurity rose to the surface as the days passed.

At one point she took a knife and threatened to stab herself through the heart unless David chose between them.

Their original plan had been to kill Noelene within hours of her abduction, yet here she was three days later very much alive. However, time was running out for the bar manager. Catherine's nagging, tears and threats all had their effect. David forced sleeping pills down Noelene's throat and then he strangled her as she slept. When they buried the body with the others, Catherine made a point of throwing dirt into the dead woman's face.

The next day, David and a very relieved Catherine were back on the road looking for their next victim. They found one in 21-year-old Denise Brown, who was walking home from visiting a friend. Her fate matched those of the Birnies' previous victims.

Corpse in the back seat

By this time, the couple had devised a fixed method of abduction. The victim would be lured into the car and threatened with a knife before being tied and gagged. However, they were not always successful. On the day after they abducted Denise, they offered a lift to a young university student as she was walking home from her classes. The offer was turned down because the girl wanted the exercise. As the Birnies tried to change the girl's mind, she noticed a person slumped in the back seat. She seemed to be sleeping.

It was Denise Brown. She was being driven to her death.

After the Birnies had failed to lure the university student into their car, they drove to a nearby pine plantation. Once there, David raped Denise twice. He stabbed her in the neck during the second assault, but when he stood up Catherine handed him a larger knife – she was not convinced that their captive was dead. Holding a flashlight, she looked on as David stabbed Denise repeatedly.

When he had finished, they prepared yet another shallow grave. But Denise was not dead. As the Birnies began to cover up what they thought was a corpse, the terrified girl sat up. David was stunned, but the shock was not enough to prevent him from grabbing an axe and striking his victim yet again. He hit the girl with all the force he could muster, but she sat up

Catherine Birnie leaves the Supreme Court in Perth after being sentenced to spend the rest of her life in jail

again just as the couple had gone back to burying her. This time, David brought the axe squarely down on her head, which split the young woman's skull in two. In the end, Denise Brown was buried just like the others.

Three days after Denise's grisly death, on the evening of 9 November, David and Catherine abducted their fifth victim, a 16-year-old girl whose identity is protected. She would bring their killing spree to an end. Her early hours at 3 Moorhouse Street matched the horrors experienced by the other victims. She was raped repeatedly as Catherine watched.

Next morning, Catherine untied her after David had left for his job at the scrap yard. She was then forced to telephone her parents. Catherine told her to tell them that she was staying with friends. Shortly afterwards, Catherine left the room to deal with someone who had arrived at the front door. She returned to find that her captive had escaped through an open window. Before the morning was over a number of police officers were standing outside the Birnie house.

There was no one there, so they waited. Catherine was arrested on kidnapping charges as she arrived home and David was picked up at his job.

Both of them denied kidnapping the girl. They insisted that she had willingly accompanied them to 3 Moorhouse Street in order to take the drugs they had offered.

David admitted having sex with her, but he continued to claim that the act was consensual. He stuck to his story through many hours of questioning. At the same time, he denied having anything to do with the recent spate of missing girls and women.

When David finally admitted the truth, it was in an unexpected way. The afternoon had passed and the evening was setting in,

David Birnie is led from court in handcuffs, 11 February 1987

but no progress had been made. Suddenly a detective came out with a half-joking statement.

'It's getting dark. Best we take the shovel and dig them up.'

'Okay. There's four of them,' came David's reply.

After learning that David had confessed, Catherine too began to speak. She gave an explanation for her sloppiness in allowing the girl to escape earlier in the day:

> *'I think I must have come to a decision that, sooner or later, there had to be an end to the rampage. I had reached the stage when I didn't know what to do. I suppose I came to a decision that I was prepared to give her a chance... I had a great fear that I would have to look at another killing like that of Denise Brown, the girl he murdered with an axe. I wanted to avoid that at all costs. In the back of my mind I had come to the position where I really did not care if the girl escaped or not.'*

It was 35 days after the first murder and Catherine was weary of the killings.

On 10 February 1987 David was taken to the Perth Supreme Court, where he pleaded guilty to the murders of Mary Neilson, Susannah Candy, Noelene Patterson and Denise Brown. He was sentenced to life imprisonment.

He last saw Catherine on 3 March, the day of her sentencing. The pair stood holding hands when Catherine learned that she too would be spending the rest of her life in prison. Although they were denied visiting privileges and telephone calls, David and Catherine kept in close contact by writing thousands of letters to each other.

The outcome

In the early hours of 2 October 2005, David Birnie was found hanging in his cell. He was 55 years old. It was the day before he was due to appear in court on charges of raping a fellow prisoner.

Catherine was denied permission to attend his funeral. She applied for parole in 2007, but this too was denied. Two years later, Catherine Birnie earned the distinction of being the third woman in Australia to have her documentation flagged 'NEVER TO BE RELEASED'.

JERRY BRUDOS
The Fetishist's Workshop

For most of his 67 years, Jerome Henry Brudos was simply called 'Jerry', but he would become famous as 'The Shoe Fetish Slayer' and 'The Lust Killer'. Neither appellation really fits – for one, his fetishes extended far beyond footwear. What is more, both nicknames suggest that Jerry's crimes extended no further than murder when in fact he was a torturer and a rapist, with an attraction toward necrophilia.

Brudos was born on 31 January 1939, in the small South Dakota town of Webster. Times were hard for his family. They had suffered under the weight of the Great Depression for nearly a decade. Not long after welcoming the new baby, they gave up on their farm and moved to Oregon, but the move did not bring the financial stability they had hoped for. Jerry's father, Henry, was forced to work at two jobs and he had little time to spend with the family.

When he was not at school, Jerry was usually with his domineering, stern mother, Eileen. It's strange that this is so – Eileen didn't like Jerry. She much preferred her eldest son, Larry, on whom she constantly doted.

Her resentment of Jerry can be traced back to his birth. As the mother of three sons she had desperately wanted her fourth child to be a girl, but Jerry had arrived instead. He grew up feeling that his mother was not happy about his gender.

Eileen's disappointment with Jerry's sex might explain a rather curious incident from his early life. At the age of 5, he found a pair of elegant women's high-heeled shoes at the local dump. He began wearing them in secret around the house, but his mother soon saw what he was doing. She flew into a rage and then she insisted that he get rid of the feminine footwear. When she discovered that Jerry had not done as she requested, she doused the offending items with petrol and set them alight. Then she forced Jerry to watch as the forbidden footwear went up in flames.

Whatever Eileen's intention might have been, it is more than likely that she furthered her son's interest in women's footwear. In short, it was the attraction to the forbidden. Not long afterwards, Jerry was caught trying to steal his nursery school teacher's shoes.

By 1955 the Great Depression and the hardship it had caused seemed far away. The Brudos family had moved into an attractive middle-class home in a pleasant neighbourhood. Now 16 years old, Jerry found himself living next door to a couple with three teenage daughters. He not only spied on the girls from the windows of his home, but he began stealing their underwear from the clothes line.

After the theft of the missing articles had been reported to the police, Jerry saw an opportunity to further his increasingly unusual desire for things feminine. He began by convincing one of the girls that he was working on the crime with the police and then he invited her over to discuss the case. When the girl appeared, Jerry invited her in and then he excused himself and left the room. He returned wearing a mask. Suddenly he held a knife to her throat and forced her to strip.

Once her clothes were on the floor Jerry took a number of photographs before leaving the room. He reappeared just as his neighbour was about to flee. Before she could raise the alarm, he quickly explained that a masked man had locked him up. It was a bold story, a ridiculous story, yet the girl told no one about the bizarre and terrifying experience.

Nude photographs

Not long afterwards an emboldened Jerry began beating another girl after she had refused to strip for him, but he was interrupted by an elderly couple who happened to be out for a stroll. The police were called, a report was made and an investigation began. They soon found Jerry's shoe collection, the stolen lingerie and the nude photographs he had taken of his neighbour.

Jerry was sent to the psychiatric ward at Oregon State Hospital, where he related his fantasies to the psychiatrists. One of them involved an underground prison. He dreamt of a place in which he could keep captured girls. That way, he would be able to have any girl he wanted, whenever he wanted.

The psychiatrists were not concerned by what they were hearing, because they believed that Jerry's dark sexual desires would pass with adolescence. The same psychiatrists determined that Jerry was borderline schizophrenic, yet after nine months at the hospital he was discharged. Tests revealed that Jerry was an intelligent person, yet he lacked motivation and self-discipline. When he graduated from high school he ended up very close to the bottom of his class.

Jerry gave no thought to university. Instead he looked for a job, but he found nothing.

Sexual fantasies

Having come to a dead end he set his sights on a military career, but he was soon discharged as an undesirable recruit after sharing his sexual fantasies with an army psychiatrist. Forced to return home, he lapsed into his old habits. He not only began stealing shoes and underwear but he also went back to assaulting women. Taking things a stage further he tried to abduct one young woman, but when she lost consciousness Jerry stole her shoes instead.

By 1961 Jerry had become an electronics technician. While he was working at a local radio station he took up with an attractive girl named Ralphene. The 17-year-old liked the idea of dating a man who was five years her senior. At the age of 23, Jerry finally lost his virginity. It was not long before Ralphene became pregnant, so with considerable reluctance her parents agreed to a wedding.

The ceremony took place in the spring of 1962, but there was not much of a honeymoon. Ralphene soon discovered that her new husband was very controlling. What is more, his requests were really peculiar. Jerry insisted that his bride do all her housework in the nude... except for a pair of high-heeled shoes, of course. Jerry also forbade Ralphene to enter his basement. Unbeknown to his wife, Jerry spent his time printing photographs of Ralphene wearing the articles of women's clothing that he had stolen over the years.

Ralphene was young and inexperienced when the couple were first married, so she went along with her husband's unusual requests, but as time went on she became more assertive. No longer was Jerry's wife willing to be photographed, no longer would she don the underwear he gave her. The housework was now done in an overall. She was a mother now, with another child on the way. Now that Ralphene was no longer an outlet for his sexual fantasies, Jerry turned inwards. He began wearing his collection of stolen women's underwear on a daily basis, often under his work clothes.

Things escalated dramatically one evening, shortly after the birth of his second child. Quite by chance Jerry spotted a very attractive woman walking down a street in Portland. He followed her to her apartment and then he stood and watched her windows. The hours went by, but Jerry did not move until he was certain that she had gone to sleep. He then broke in. The woman woke up just as he was in the process of stealing her underwear, so he jumped on the bed and raped her.

Frustrated by Ralphene's refusal to participate in his fantasies, Jerry took photographs of himself in women's clothing and then he left them around the house. When they were ignored, he retreated into his basement workshop. Jerry had already committed rape, but his sexual fantasies were about to manifest themselves in an even more violent fashion.

On 26 January 1968 he committed his first murder. His victim, 19-year-old Linda Slawson, was trying to fund her education as a door-to-door encyclopedia saleswoman. When she approached Jerry in his garden he expressed great enthusiasm, so she willingly

Victim Linda J. Slawson was trying to work her way through college by selling encyclopedias door to door

followed him into his basement so that she could continue her sales pitch. Once inside, she was clubbed on the head and strangled.

When he was certain that Linda was dead, he went upstairs, peeled some bills from his wallet and sent his family out to a local fast food restaurant. Once they had left, he began acting out his fantasies with the dead woman's body. But Jerry did not stop when his wife and children returned – in fact, he continued with his activities for several days.

He then dipped into his collection of shoes and women's underwear so that he could dress Linda's body in high heels and lingerie. Numerous photographs were taken, the articles of clothing would be changed and the cycle would be repeated. Jerry also had sex with Linda's body. After a few days of exhausting activity he took the corpse to the Willamette River and threw it from a bridge. Before doing so, he cut off one of Linda's feet with a hacksaw and placed it in the basement freezer. From time to time, Jerry would place a shoe on the severed foot and then masturbate. When the severed foot had almost rotted away, Brudos threw it into the river to join the corpse.

Jerry did not kill again until several months later. In the intervening period he moved his family to Salem, Oregon's state capital. The new Brudos home was rather unattractive, but it did have one feature that appealed to the head of the household – a separate garage. Located off a narrow roadway, the structure would serve as Jerry's new workshop. It would be much more private than the basement.

Hung from a meat hook

On the evening of 26 November 1968 Jerry abducted Jan Whitney, his second murder victim. The family had not even settled in at that point. He had come across the young woman on Interstate 5 (I-5), after spotting her broken-down car. The vehicle could be fixed, or so he claimed, but first he had to return to his home to retrieve some tools. Jan went back to Salem with Jerry. Once there, Jerry raped and strangled her in the passenger seat of the family car.

During the next five days, Jan's body hung from a meat hook in Jerry's garage. He dressed the corpse, took photographs and committed acts of necrophilia, as before. Then he took a break by going off on a Thanksgiving weekend getaway with his wife and family. While the Brudos family were away a freak accident very nearly exposed Jan's dangling corpse and with it Jerry's secret life. A car spun out of control and hit his garage with such force that it made a large crack in the wooden structure, which brought several police officers to the scene. Had they bothered to look through the damaged wall they would have seen Jan Whitney's hanging body.

The close call served to embolden Jerry. He thought he was so clever that he could do whatever he pleased without being caught. A few days after his return, Jerry disposed of Jan's corpse in the Willamette River. Before doing so he cut off her right breast, intending to use it as a mould for making paperweights. He would be frustrated in his attempts.

Linda Slawson's work had led her to approach Jerry, while Jan Whitney's murder was the result of a chance encounter – now, however, Jerry was ready to stalk his prey. Dressed in women's clothing, he hung around in a Salem department store parking garage and on 27 March 1969 he abducted his next victim. Jerry did not kill 19-year-old Karen Sprinker immediately. Instead he forced her to model various items from his collection of women's clothing. After he became tired of that game he put a noose around her neck, raised her a few inches above the ground and left his garage workshop to join his family for dinner. When he returned, Karen was dead. He cut off both of her breasts in yet another attempt at making a paperweight and then he threw her into the Long Tom River.

Less than a month later, Jerry was hunting for a new victim. On 21 April he attacked another young woman, Sharon Wood, in a parking garage. A struggle ensued, Sharon bit Jerry's thumb and he ran. A few days later he tried again, this time choosing a much younger target. As 12-year-old Gloria Smith walked to school, he approached her with a fake pistol and began marching her to his car. Fortunately Gloria showed quick thinking by running to a woman who was working in her garden.

Fake police badge

Jerry had thought himself so clever, but he had now failed on two occasions. He had even been outwitted by a young girl. Clearly he needed more than an imitation pistol if his abductions were going to be successful. So Jerry went out and bought a fake police badge, which he used to abduct Linda Salee, his final victim. He approached the young woman in a Portland shopping centre car park and accused her of shoplifting. After meekly following his orders, Linda was driven back to his Salem garage where she was tied up. Jerry then had dinner in the house with his family.

On his return, he was surprised to find that Linda had removed the ropes. The young woman was free and yet she had not fled, so Jerry tied her up a second time and suspended her from the ceiling. After undressing her and taking a series of photographs, he hanged her.

Linda was Jerry's fourth murder victim and yet the police had not linked the murders together. In fact, they did not even know that the women were dead. Jerry might have gone on killing for some time had it not been for an angler's discovery.

Jerry Brudos, 30, leaves Marion County Circuit Courtroom after changing his plea to guilty

On 10 May 1969, roughly a month after Linda's murder, the man spotted her body floating in the Long Tom River. Two days later, police divers found Karen Sprinker's remains. They were just a few feet away from Linda's corpse.

Jerry was unconcerned when the news raced through the community. He was confident that nothing could link him to the bodies.

He was wrong.

When Jerry had tied the women up he had used an unusual knot, one that was often used by electricians when they pulled wires through a house. The knot would tie Jerry to the murders.

The police then visited the campus of Oregon State University, where Karen Sprinker had been a student. They were told stories about a peculiar man who had been seen roaming the campus. One young woman had even had a date with the man.

When he called again, the police were waiting. It was Jerry Brudos. A background check revealed Jerry's occupation and his history of attacking teenage girls, so detectives paid a visit to the Brudos home.

They noticed a piece of rope in Jerry's garage. It was identical to the one that had been tied around the two bodies that had been found in the Long Tom River. Recognizing the investigators' interest, the ever-bold Jerry offered them a sample. It later proved to be a perfect match.

Closing in

Jerry could sense that the police were closing in, so on 30 May he made for the Canadian border, accompanied by his wife. The couple were spotted by the Oregon State Police. Although Jerry was arrested on the relatively minor charge of armed assault in relation to 12-year-old Gloria Smith, he became talkative in custody. He took great pleasure in providing very detailed accounts of the murders that he had committed. At the same time he showed no remorse, telling one detective that the women he had abused and killed were nothing more than objects to him. In fact, he went so far as to compare each of the dead women to a candy wrapper.

'Once you're done with them, you just discard them. Why would you not discard them? You don't have any more use for them.'

On 27 June, Jerry pleaded guilty to all of the charges that had been made against him. He received three life sentences amounting to at least 36 years in prison. Jerry became eligible for parole in 2005, but as the years passed and the date of his release approached it became increasingly clear that he would never again be a free man.

He died of liver cancer on 29 March 2006, at the age of 67.

ARIEL CASTRO
The Bus Driver's Home-made Lock-up

On 22 August 2002, 21-year-old Michelle Knight was on her way to a social services meeting to talk about custody of her son, Joey. She was late and in a rush. So when a man, who she recognized as the father of a girl at Joey's school, came up to her and offered her a lift, she happily accepted. He began driving the wrong way. They pulled up on to his driveway. He said he was just going to get a puppy for Joey, so innocently Knight followed him in, only a little suspicious. He took her up to the second floor, shut the door and locked it. So began Michelle Knight's 11 years in hell.

Bad husband

Ariel Castro was born in San Juan, Puerto Rico on 10 July 1960. As a child he moved with his divorced mother and three siblings to Reading, Pennsylvania and then to Cleveland. His father, Pedro, worked as a car dealer in a tough neighbourhood. When he lived in Puerto Rico, one of his arms had been chopped off with a machete in a gang dispute.

Castro met his wife, Grimilda Figueroa, in the 1980s. She lived in the house opposite and their relationship blossomed. In 1992 they moved into a house on Seymour Avenue. That was when things started to go wrong. It turned out Castro had a violent streak a mile wide.

He began beating his wife, breaking her nose, ribs and arms. He threw her down a flight of stairs and she suffered a skull fracture as a result. In 1993 he was arrested for domestic violence but managed to avoid a conviction. Grimilda moved away with her four children in 1996, leaving Castro to rattle around his house alone.

Ariel Castro's house on Seymour Avenue, now demolished

Castro worked as a bus driver. He could be counted no more successful in his working life than in the domestic sphere. He had a strange idea of what his job entailed. He would use the bus to do his grocery shopping, leave passengers on the bus while he left for lunch, and he also made an illegal U-turn with children on his bus. In 2004, he was charged with child endangerment and abduction after the incident.

Anonymous call

In April 2003 Amanda Berry's mother received a call from her daughter's phone. A male voice spoke: 'I have Amanda. She's fine and will be coming home in a couple of weeks.' Berry, a 16-year-old girl, had gone to work as normal at the local Burger King on 21 April 2003. Leaving at 7:30 pm, she called her sister to tell her, 'I've got a ride, I'll call you back.'

The lift was with Ariel Castro, who by this time was already holding Michelle Knight prisoner. In 2004, 14-year-old Georgina 'Gina' Lynn DeJesus also went missing. She had been on her way home from school. Gina thought she was being dropped off by Castro – she was friends with his daughter at school. The two teenagers had joined Michelle Knight in captivity.

A widespread search was to prove fruitless. Local police and FBI could find no clue as to the girls' whereabouts. Knight's disappearance was not considered a high priority as she was an adult. An 'AMBER' alert (standing for America's Missing: Broadcast Emergency Response) was never issued for Gina's disappearance, though it is not clear why since this is standard procedure. Nonetheless, the disappearances soon attracted widespread attention.

The two younger girls featured prominently on American TV. A segment on the programme *America's Most Wanted*, putting out the alert for Berry and DeJesus, was aired over and over between 2004 and 2006.

The FBI released a composite sketch of the suspect that, apart from the age range, captured Ariel Castro pretty well. It described a Latino, 25 to 35 years old, 5 feet 10, 165 to 185 pounds, with green eyes and a goatee. Castro fitted the profile; he was 43 at the time, 5 foot 7, weighing in at 179 pounds with green eyes and a goatee. Yet somehow he did not come in for detailed investigation at the time.

Vigils were held and searches made for the two younger girls. Castro even participated in these and tried to get close to the family. It helped him to strengthen his reputation as an upstanding member of the community, but secretly he enjoyed witnessing their pain as he held their loved ones captive. More disturbingly perhaps, he wrote an article on Gina DeJesus's disappearance for Cleveland's west side newspaper, the Plain Press.

Despite the efforts of police and community, it would be another decade before the captives saw freedom.

Chained up

Ariel Castro had turned his house into an amateur prison. Makeshift alarms had been attached to the front and back doors. Padlocks, bolts and ordinary locks were everywhere. He had an endless supply of duct tape, metal chains and plastic zip-ties to keep his prisoners restrained. His son, Anthony, noticed there were parts of the house that were always locked – the attic, the basement, the garage. During one of his visits, just a few weeks before their escape, Castro asked his son if he thought Amanda Berry would ever be found. Anthony replied that he thought they were dead. Castro gave him an eerie reply: 'Really? You think so?'

Captivity in the house at 2207 Seymour Avenue was a hellish experience. When Knight was first kidnapped, her hands and feet were tied together and she was left for three days before Castro fed her. Later, the three women were repeatedly raped. On the worst days, this could occur up to five times. For her 17th birthday, Amanda Berry was forced to shower with her tormentor. He then locked her to a pole in the basement and chains were tied around her stomach. A trash can was left nearby to be used as her 'bathroom'.

On 27 April she wrote an entry in her diary:

It's Sunday. I've been gone six days. And so far he's raped me at least twenty-five times.

Only the memory of her mother and a close relationship with her fellow victims kept her going. Amanda took the pictures of her mother from the wallet and fashioned a frame for them out of torn pieces of a cereal box. It was something to cling on to in the face of so much provocation. 'I'm not here to kill you. I don't want to kill you! This is just about my sexual problem,' Castro told her.

Occasionally when he raped her he would take the cord from a vacuum cleaner and tighten it around her neck. The memory of her mother helped her to get through the ordeal:

When he is doing horrible things to my body, I look at my mum's face … I look into her eyes and lose myself in her. And my mom and I get through it.

The new normal

Beatings were commonplace in Castro's house. During an interview on ABC after her release, Gina DeJesus recalled her torment. 'He seems angry, like he wants to hurt me as much as he can. I'm screaming and crying and beating him back, but it's useless.'

Even when they weren't facing abuse themselves they were forced to watch as the other women suffered.

Knight and Berry were made pregnant by Castro. The physical abuse Castro administered to Knight, including starving her and punching her in the stomach, led to multiple miscarriages while she was in captivity.

In Amanda Berry's case, she was forced to bear Castro's child in 2006, a daughter, Jocelyn. Michelle helped Amanda deliver her baby in a paddling pool. The captives tried to shield Jocelyn from the gruesome reality of their situation. They created a kindergarten in their one-room prison for the little girl. When she turned five, they even came up with the idea of a 'walk to school'.

They would all pretend to leave the house, cross the road, and then sit Jocelyn down at a desk. Amanda would then pretend to be a teacher. She even created schoolwork for her daughter to try and give her some sense of a normal life.

Similarly, Ariel Castro acted quite surprisingly towards Jocelyn. Paradoxically, he too was trying to give his daughter some sense of normality. He pretended they were a real family and would take the little girl to church. He bought her toys and clothes while her mother was left at home in chains.

Mental torture

The abuse went beyond physical torment. Castro seemed to delight in their mental anguish. At one point he gave Amanda a local newspaper to read. In it was an article in which her mother spoke about how worried she was. In March 2006, Amanda learned her mother had died while she was watching the TV news. Castro even attacked the fragile bonds that held the victims together. He would tell them he had called their families to tell them they were now his girlfriends, but even at his most cruel he would always give them hope that they might be released soon. He would tell them they would be leaving in a 'few months'. At one point Amanda threatened to kill herself. Castro simply handed her a noose and told her that he would bury her corpse in the backyard.

At first, the girls got along well with each other. Gina and Amanda remained close throughout the ordeal, but over time their relations with Michelle became strained. Castro would play mind games. He would lie to them, saying that he did not have sex with the other girls in order to turn them against each other. Sometimes one girl would be privileged over the others. Gina DeJesus said it drove the girls apart: 'It could be from getting more food, less food, different clothes. It was just simple things, but when you don't have anything, you're like, "Well, why don't I have that?"'

On 6 May, 2013, the three prisoners' ordeal finally ended. Amanda's daughter, Jocelyn, noticed Castro was no longer in the house. For once, he had forgotten to lock the screen door that kept them trapped in their single-room prison.

At first, they thought it was a trick. In the past, Castro had left areas of the house unlocked, and if they attempted to escape, he would beat them.

Amanda could take it no longer – she seized the opportunity. She saw neighbours outside the door and began screaming. They

Michelle Knight addresses the court in 2013 as Castro bows his head in the background

helped her kick a hole through the front door. Finally, she was able to do what she had been trying to for nearly a decade. She made the call to 911:

> *Help me. I'm Amanda Berry. I've been kidnapped and I've been missing for 10 years.*

Inside the house the police found DeJesus and Knight huddled together in the bathroom. Knight flew into the arms of one of the police officers saying 'You saved me' again and again. They were taken to MetroHealth Medical Center and could finally begin their return to normal life.

The details of their captivity were soon well known around the world. It became an international media sensation. Reports

Castro protested to the judge before being sentenced: 'I'm not a monster. I'm sick... but I'm a happy person inside'

dominated coverage of the *Cleveland Plain Dealer, the Daily Mail, CNN* and *ABC.* DeJesus and Berry wrote a book together revealing all the horrific details of their captivity simply called *Hope.*

Castro was charged with 977 counts of kidnapping, rape, and aggravated murder among other crimes. He pleaded guilty to 937 of them and received a sentence of 1,000 years without parole. He was spared the death penalty as part of his plea deal. Michelle Knight spoke at the sentencing: 'I spent 11 years in hell, and your hell is just beginning'.

Castro's house in Seymour Avenue has now been demolished. He is no longer with us either. Just 30 days into his sentence, he hanged himself with a bedsheet in his cell at Pickaway Correctional Institution.

JOHN REGINALD CHRISTIE
The House in the Cul-de-sac

Number 10 Rillington Place was located in a cul-de-sac in the Notting Hill area of London. The unremarkable three-storey house was run down and very grey, yet it came to rival 10 Downing Street as Britain's most famous address. While Sir Winston Churchill occupied the prime minister's residence, the other 'Number 10' was home to the most prolific British serial killer of the first half of the 20th century.

John Reginald Halliday Christie seemed such an ordinary man. Born in Halifax, West Yorkshire on 8 April 1899, he was the son of a carpet designer. The childhood he shared with his six siblings was strict and lacking in affection, but was not unusual for the late-Victorian and Edwardian period. For the most part the young Christie kept to himself, concentrating on his studies. His efforts were rewarded when he was awarded a scholarship to Halifax Secondary School at the age of 11, where his favourite subject was mathematics. Though he was a promising student, Christie ended his studies four years later, after taking a job as an assistant film projectionist.

Christie enlisted in the army at the age of 17, shortly after the First World War had entered its third year. In April 1918 he was sent to France, where he served as a signal officer. Two months later, he was badly injured in a mustard gas attack. Christie would claim that he had been blinded and rendered mute by the attack. While both claims were false, he spoke in a whisper for the remainder of his adult life.

Christie's relationships with women were hindered by his impotence. His condition was no secret, earning him the nicknames 'Reggie-No-Dick' and 'Can't-Do-It-Christie'. However, he discovered that he could perform with prostitutes, so he continued to use their services even after his May 1920 marriage to Ethel Waddington. Less than a year into the marriage, the young groom received the first of his many criminal convictions after stealing money orders while he was working for the Royal Mail. His earliest crimes only resulted in probation, but by 1924 he had begun moving in and out of prison.

Assault on a prostitute

Two of Christie's many early offences stand out. In May 1929, close to his ninth wedding anniversary, he was sentenced to six months' hard labour for striking a prostitute on the head with a

Badly injured in a mustard gas attack, Christie spoke in a whisper for the rest of his life

cricket bat. Four years later, he was found guilty of stealing the car of a priest who had befriended him. Christie's early criminal activities seemed to come to a halt with this last crime, for which he served a three-month jail sentence.

As 1938 came to a close the Christies moved into 10 Rillington Place, a run-down building on a street that had seen better days, where they occupied the ground-floor flat and cellar. The house was a throwback to an earlier time. It consisted of three separate flats, one per storey, all without bathrooms. The tenants shared a single toilet, which was outside in the back garden. Nine months after moving in, Christie found a new job. The Second World War had just begun and the 40-year-old had been accepted into the Special Constabulary. It was a position of authority for which he was clearly unqualified, yet no one had bothered to check his background.

Christie was assigned to the Harrow Road police station. Despite his ongoing sexual dysfunction, he soon began having an affair with one of the women who worked in the canteen. The relationship continued until her husband returned from the war. Shortly afterwards, in August 1943, Christie committed his first murder. Taking advantage of the fact that his wife was out of town, he took Ruth Fuerst, a prostitute, back to the Rillington Place flat, where he strangled her during sex.

'I left her there in the bedroom,' he later told investigators. 'After that, I believe I had a cup of tea and went to bed.'

For a brief period of time Christie stored Ruth's body under the floorboards in the front room, eventually burying her in the garden.

Christie abruptly resigned from the Special Constabulary, though he gave no reason. Was it because he felt guilty after committing murder? Or did it have something to do with his affair with the woman in the canteen? Whatever the cause, Christie took another job, this time as a clerk at a radio factory.

His second victim was co-worker Muriel Eady, who met her end in October 1944. First of all Christie lured her to his apartment with the promise of a concoction that would cure her bronchitis and then he persuaded her to inhale from a jar containing Friar's Balsam. The pungent solution hid the smell that was created when Christie inserted a gas pipe into the jar. When Muriel lost consciousness she was raped and then strangled to death.

Five years passed before the next murders took place at 10 Rillington Place. But was Christie responsible? The bodies of Beryl Evans and her 1-year-old daughter Geraldine, Christie's upstairs neighbours, had been found in the garden's washhouse by grieving husband and father Timothy Evans. Or so he claimed. Evans then pointed an accusing finger at Christie. He said that his neighbour had killed his wife while attempting to perform an illegal abortion. Why the abortionist had killed Geraldine was a mystery to the young man.

Under intense questioning, Evans changed his story. This time he told the police that he was the one who had killed his wife and his daughter. He later withdrew his confession. Christie was the true murderer, he declared.

Evans was put on trial for the death of his daughter on 11 January 1950, while his wife's murder was left 'on file'. The prosecution's case relied heavily on the testimony of the crown's key witness – John Reginald Halliday Christie. Evans was found guilty and he was hanged on 9 March.

The next person to be murdered at 10 Rillington Place was

Ethel Christie. She had been married to her husband for over 32 years when he strangled her on 14 December 1952. The event kick-started a three-month killing spree, during which three more women were murdered – Kathleen Maloney, Rita Nelson and Hectorina Maclennan. In all three cases Christie used gas to make each of his victims drowsy before raping them. He then strangled them with a piece of rope.

Christie kept the three bodies in his flat, hiding them in a kitchen alcove. From time to time, he would commit acts of necrophilia. He was very nearly exposed when one of his fellow tenants stole some produce from a local grocer and was chased back to 10 Rillington Place. After the man was arrested, a police inspector stood chatting to Christie:

'I said to him, "What a rotten smell there is in your house, Christie". And he said to me, "It's all those blooming tenants upstairs". I didn't realize at that time that I was standing in the front room with his mouldering wife underneath the floorboards where we were standing.'

Now 51 years old, Christie was unemployed and living off what he had taken from Ethel's bank account. He had even gone so far as to pawn her wedding ring and her few pieces of jewellery.

On 20 March he was desperate for cash, so he sublet his flat for roughly £8 a week and walked out of 10 Rillington Place for the last time. Though Christie had made little attempt to hide the bodies of his three final victims, four days passed before they were discovered.

While the police were investigating the property they found the bodies that Christie had buried in the garden, along with

A pipe-smoking man carries a parcel of human remains from 10 Rillington Place to a waiting police van

a Gold Leaf tobacco tin containing the pubic hair that he had clipped from his victims.

After a six-day manhunt, Christie was spotted on an embankment near Putney Bridge. When he was arrested, his only possessions were a few coins and some old newspaper clippings about Timothy Evans.

Terrible confession

Christie admitted killing seven women, including Beryl Evans, but he never confessed to the murder of Geraldine Evans. In the end he was tried for only one murder, that of his wife Ethel. Standing in the very courtroom in which Timothy Evans had been sentenced to death, Christie pleaded insanity. However, the jury was not convinced and he was found guilty.

By the time he was hanged on 15 July 1953, plans were already in motion to erase 10 Rillington Place from the public memory. The house would remain standing, but the name of the cul-de-sac, with all of its hideous associations, would soon be changed to Ruston Close. In 1971, 18 years after the final murder, the squalid building was pulled down as part of a large-scale redevelopment of the area. Today, no building stands on the land that was once occupied by 10 Rillington Place.

JEFFREY DAHMER
The Foul-smelling Apartment

As a child, Jeffrey Lionel Dahmer was fascinated by the internal organs of animals. He spent many hours each week riding around his community, Ohio's Bath Township, on the lookout for roadkill. He took pleasure in cutting open the dead animals he found. It gave him a sense of power, a feeling of control. As an adult Jeffrey would seek power and control over people, not animals. It was a goal that led to rape, torture, murder, necrophilia, cannibalism and failed attempts to make 'living zombies'.

Jeffrey was born in the Milwaukee County suburb of West Allis on 21 May 1960. His parents, Lionel and Joyce Dahmer, were comfortably off because of Lionel's work as a chemist, but they constantly bickered.

When things became heated, Jeffrey would often withdraw into a fantasy world in which things were more stable. Nevertheless, he always maintained that his childhood had been a very happy one.

According to Jeffrey, his fascination with the inner workings of animals had been triggered by a ninth-grade biology class, in which he had been asked to dissect the foetus of a pig. He took the remains home, so that he could study them further. He then set up a secret workspace in the forest that backed on to the Dahmer property, where he would dismember roadkill. When the creature had served its purpose he would bury it, thus creating a small but densely populated cemetery.

However, he chose to keep some animal parts on display – a severed dog's head, for example, which he mounted on a stake.

Sick fantasies

Jeffrey's obsession with dead animals coincided with the emergence of some very dark desires. He started to have fantasies in which sex was mixed with terrible violence.

'I didn't know how to tell anyone about it,' he would later say, 'so I didn't. I just kept it all inside.'

Jeffrey was never able to identify where his sinister thoughts came from.

He often fantasized about picking up a male hitchhiker, taking him captive and doing with him whatever he wished. His dream became reality a month after his 18th birthday. As he was driving home he spotted 19-year-old Steven Hicks, who was trying to thumb a ride. At first, Jeffrey drove straight past the young man because he was afraid of the desires that were welling up within him, but then he turned his car around. Steven willingly jumped into Jeffrey's car and the pair of them drove to the Dahmer home, where they drank beer and had sex – after which Jeffrey clubbed Steven to death with a barbell. It was then that he got to cut open a human body for the first time. The experience was just as pleasurable as he had imagined. He liked the feel of Steven's insides, particularly as they were still warm. The hitchhiker's body was then cut into small pieces, which were placed in rubbish bags. Steven's remains were buried next to the pet cemetery.

It is more than likely that Jeffrey drank more than just a few beers with Steven on that summer night, because he had been drinking heavily since his mid-teens. His excessive drinking had begun when his disturbing fantasies were beginning to take root. The problem had affected his grades in high school and it would have a worse effect on him as time went by.

At his father's urging, Jeffrey enrolled at Ohio State University, but he ended up spending his one and only semester in a drunken haze. In frustration, Lionel Dahmer drove his son to an army recruiting office. After two years of service, Jeffrey's continuous drinking brought about his discharge.

He then returned to Ohio, where he was soon arrested for being drunk and disorderly. Desperate for some sort of solution, he went off to live with his grandmother in West Allis, but his behaviour and his drinking only got worse. Just months after moving into the elderly woman's home, an intoxicated Jeffrey dropped his trousers at the Wisconsin State Fair. He was arrested for public exposure. In September 1986 he was arrested again on the same charge, after having masturbated in front of two young boys. He was put on probation for one year.

Jeffrey was still on probation on 15 September 1987, when he committed his second murder. He picked up his victim, a 26-year-old man named Steven Tuomi, in a downtown Milwaukee gay bar. The two men rented a room in a cheap hotel, where they continued their drinking. Jeffrey put sleeping pills in Steven's drink, before passing out.

When he awoke the next morning he found that Steven had been beaten to death. It appears that he had no memory of what had taken place. Using a large suitcase, he moved Steven's body to his grandmother's basement. He then had sex with the corpse several times, before cutting it apart. Steven Tuomi's remains were left on the pavement, ready for the rubbish collection.

'After the second time,' Jeffrey later said, referring to the murder, 'the compulsion was too strong. I didn't even try to stop it after that.'

Four months later he killed Jamie Doxtator, a 14-year-old who was known to hang around outside Milwaukee's gay establishments. Then on 24 March it was 25-year-old Richard Guerrero's turn to be murdered.

By this time, Jeffrey, now 27, had been living with his grandmother for nearly six years. Her patience and understanding had been constantly tested in that time. She did not like his late nights and she thought that his behaviour was becoming increasingly bizarre. On one occasion she had come across a male mannequin in his wardrobe and on another she had stumbled across a .375 Magnum revolver under his bed.

And then there were all of those strange smells coming from her basement. Jeffrey explained that the foul odour came from a dead squirrel that had been dissolved in acid.

In the summer of 1988, Jeffrey's grandmother asked him to leave her house. He moved into a slightly ramshackle apartment in Milwaukee, but he did not live alone for long. He was arrested just a few days later for having drugged and molested a 13-year-old boy. As he awaited trial, Jeffrey returned to his grandmother's house. On 25 March 1989 he drugged and strangled a young man named Anthony Sears in her basement. Jeffrey kept the corpse there for several days, using it as a sex toy before finally dismembering it. He placed the head in boiling water, stripped off the flesh and kept it stored away until the day of his final arrest.

When his court appearance came round, Jeffrey pleaded guilty to the molestation charge. He was let out early for good behaviour and he returned to his grandmother's house as a registered sex offender.

In May 1990, just days short of his 30th birthday, Jeffrey fancied his independence again so he rented apartment 213 at 924 North 25th Street in Milwaukee. The flat would become a killing ground. A 24-year-old named Eddie Smith was murdered a month after Jeffrey moved in and three more men would die before the year was up.

Jeffrey's murders became even more frequent in the following year. He had developed an extremely effective modus operandi, which usually began with a pick-up at a gay bar or a bookshop. Back at the North 25th Street apartment, he would first drug his victims' drinks. After the pills had taken effect, he would then strangle his targets or slit their throats. By this means he achieved what he so craved – the complete control of another person.

He would then take naked photographs of the fresh corpse before having sex with it.

Next, he cut up the body. This usually happened on the same day. He ate body parts such as the biceps, the heart and the thighs, while the sexual organs were preserved in jars of formaldehyde. Copying what he did in the case of Anthony Sears, Jeffrey boiled his victims' heads clean on the stove. The skulls were then spray-painted.

Living zombies

As time went by Jeffrey gained less and less satisfaction from dismembering the bodies. His behaviour needed to become more deviant if he was to satisfy his urges. Eating the various body parts of his victims made Jeffrey feel that they were a part of him. It also gave him 'a sexual satisfaction'.

Just months before he died, Jeffrey revealed that the part he found least satisfying was the actual killing. Murder was a means to an end. What Jeffrey had desired was a person under his complete control, a person whose wishes he would not have to consider. This led to his attempts to create what he called 'living zombies'. Jeffrey would first drill into the frontal lobe of his drugged victims and then he would pour boiling water or acid through the hole. But it was all quite frustrating. Despite his best efforts the operation almost always resulted in death.

The one exception was a 14-year-old named Konerak Sinthasomphone, who escaped after Jeffrey had performed the procedure on him. It was just after midnight on 27 May 1991. The incoherent and dazed boy was walking the streets when he was approached by paramedics and the Milwaukee Police Department. By that time Jeffrey had caught up with him. He explained that the boy was his inebriated 19-year-old lover.

The police returned to Jeffrey's flat with Konerak. After taking a quick look around, they left the teenager in Jeffrey's care. Within the hour Konerak had been strangled. Jeffrey had

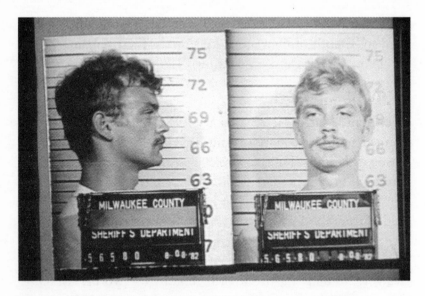

Mugshots of Jeffrey Dahmer in 1982 after being arrested for indecent exposure in Milwaukee

sex with the corpse and then began cutting it up. As usual, the boy's skull was kept as a souvenir.

The officers who had returned Konerak to Jeffrey would later recall that the North 25th Street apartment had been very neat and clean, yet it had a very unpleasant odour. Jeffrey's neighbours had also noticed the smell coming from his apartment. He apologized to them and blamed a dirty aquarium or spoiled meat.

The law finally caught up with Jeffrey on 22 July 1991, after one of his would-be victims had managed to escape from the apartment. At long last, the horrors it contained were exposed. A large drum contained a mixture of body parts floating in acid and there was a severed human head in a small freezer. The drains were full of the sludge that had been formed when he had tried to dispose of his victims by soaking their remains in acid and other chemicals.

Guilty as charged

Five months later, on 22 January 1992, Jeffrey went on trial charged with 15 counts of murder. He pleaded not guilty by reason of insanity, but two weeks later the jury returned a guilty verdict. Jeffrey was sentenced to 15 life terms or a total of 937 years in prison. Lionel visited him every month. They did not speak about the crimes. Instead, their conversations focused on the family and Jeffrey's life in prison.

When asked, Jeffrey described his life behind bars as 'slow and steady... nothing out of the ordinary'. Those words, spoken in February 1992, might have been his perception of the situation, but they were not true. He was a prime target.

In July 1994 he was attacked after attending a service in the prison chapel. Then on 28 November 1994 he died of very severe head injuries after having been beaten with an iron bar by a fellow inmate.

MARC DUTROUX
The Paedophile's Hidden Dungeon

At the turn of this past century, the actions of Marc Dutroux very nearly toppled the Belgian government. He destroyed political careers, yet had never held office himself; in fact, he wasn't even a free man. Sitting in a prison cell, his impact on the country had little connection with what he was doing, but what he had done. In 1995 and 1996, Dutroux had abducted, tortured and raped six girls, four of whom he murdered.

Dutroux was born on 6 November 1956 in the central Belgian municipality of Ixelles, but his early life was spent in the Belgian Congo, where his parents were teachers. In 1971, six years after the family returned to Belgium, Dutroux's parents divorced. Though the boy stayed with his mother, he had already started to stray from home, earning money as a male prostitute.

Marc Dutroux is led away from the house where he held so many girls captive

He married while he was still a teenager and he fathered two children with his wife. The marriage ended in 1983, partly because of Dutroux's affair with Michelle Martin.

Muggings and rape

Although Dutroux had been trained as an electrician, he derived most of his income from muggings, car theft and drug dealing. Michelle shared in all of these activities and more besides. In February 1986, she and her boyfriend were arrested and charged with kidnapping and raping five girls, but it was more than three years before they were finally convicted. In April 1989, Dutroux was given a thirteen-and-a-half year prison sentence while Michelle was sent to jail for five years. A few weeks later, the rapists were permitted to marry behind bars.

Dutroux should not have been released until the end of 2002, yet he was freed in April 1992. He was the fortunate beneficiary of a new government policy that was designed to free up the country's prisons. After his release, there was no thought of finding work as an electrician. He did much better by selling drugs and stolen cars. Not many electricians could boast of owning seven houses throughout the country.

However, it wasn't exactly business as usual. Dutroux had come across other ways of making an illegal income. For example, he managed to get a generous government pension after convincing a psychiatrist that he was unable to work. This did not come to the attention of the police until 1993, when an informant told them that he had been offered the equivalent of $5,000 (£2,500) to kidnap young girls.

Sure enough, girls had begun to go missing in several of the neighbourhoods in which the supposedly disabled electrician owned houses. Even so, the information was completely ignored. The Belgian police would continue to display an almost unbelievable level of incompetence. Innocent lives would be lost as a result.

In 1995, the same informant told the police that he had learned that Dutroux was constructing a dungeon in which he intended to hold girls captive before selling them into prostitution. That same year, Dutroux's mother told the prosecutors that her son was holding young girls in one of his vacant houses. There was indeed a dungeon. A cramped space, measuring just two metres (seven feet) in length, one metre (three feet) in width and one-and-a-half metres (five feet) in height, it was located in the cellar of 128 Avenue Phillippeville in Marcinelle, Dutroux and Michelle's primary residence. It was a fiendishly clever design, with soundproof walls and a ventilation hole in the ceiling. The police searched the house for missing girls on two separate occasions, but they did not look behind the shelves that hid the dungeon door. It was not until the third visit that they finally saw the hidden room – and this was only after Dutroux himself pointed out the door.

Interrogation

On 13 August 1996 Dutroux, Michelle and a man named Michel Lelièvre were arrested on suspicion of abducting 14-year-old Laetitia Delhez as she was walking home from a public swimming pool. A witness had identified the Dutroux's white van. After two days of intense interrogation, Dutroux confessed to the crime and revealed that the informant had been correct about his dungeon. When the police finally opened the hidden door they found two girls – Laetitia and 12-year-old Sabine

Dardenne. Sabine had been missing for almost three months. Both girls had been raped and then filmed for the purposes of child pornography.

With Dutroux's secrets finally coming to light the police quickly moved in on his other six properties, hoping that they might find more missing girls. Sadly, they were about six months too late in the case of Julie Lejeune and Melissa Russo. The two friends, both just 8 years old, had disappeared on 24 June 1995. Their bodies, and that of a man named Bernard Weinstein, were uncovered in the back garden of Dutroux's house in Sars-la-Buissière.

According to Dutroux, the two girls had starved to death in either February or March 1996, while he was serving a prison sentence for car theft. Dutroux explained that during his incarceration Weinstein had been entrusted with their care. Instead, the man had simply let the two little girls starve to death. When a newly freed Dutroux learned of Weinstein's negligence, he tortured the man by crushing his testicles. Then he drugged him with barbiturates and buried him alive beside the two girls. During their seven or eight months of captivity, Julie and Melissa were tortured, raped and made to act in pornographic films. In short, they were treated in much the same way as the other girls Dutroux had abducted.

And there were others.

On 22 August 1995 Dutroux and Lelièvre kidnapped An Marchal, aged 19, and Eefje Lambreks, aged 17, who had been camping outside the municipality of Ostend, a Belgian resort. Their bodies were found buried under the concrete floor of a shed at yet another of Dutroux's houses.

It soon became apparent that the ring of paedophiles extended far beyond Dutroux, Lelièvre and the dead Bernard Weinstein. Michelle Martin and businessman Jean-Michel Nihoul were also members. When it became known that Nihoul had once organized an adult orgy at a Belgian château, which had been attended by government officials and police officers, there was speculation that the paedophile ring might extend into some very high places. Added to that, a number of police officers were suspended because of their negligence – or their possible involvement in the scandal.

Soon there were calls for a public inquiry. The mood of the public became even more heated when in October 1996 the investigative judge in the Dutroux case, Jean-Marc Connerotte, was dismissed for attending a fund-raising dinner in aid of the search for the missing children. It was claimed that his attendance might have caused him to lose objectivity. A little over a week later, Connerotte's suspicious dismissal and the continuing stories of police incompetence led 300,000 people to march through the streets of Brussels. The Belgian public were further angered by the possibility of a government cover-up. As more evidence emerged, other forms of protest were employed.

The public transport system came to a halt when railway employees refused to work and many other workers simply walked away from their jobs. Encouraged by this show of support, the victims' families called for a general strike. The Belgian Prime Minister Jean-Luc Dehaene tried to position himself on the side of the protestors by declaring that their efforts would help speed up reforms to the justice system.

In April 1997, a parliamentary committee concluded that many, if not all, of the murdered girls might have been saved had the police not made so many errors during their investigations. Its report called for the formation of two new police organizations – one local and one national.

Daring escape

The damaged reputation of the police was further sullied 12 months later when Dutroux was allowed to leave prison so that he could consult documents that might be used in his trial. Almost within sight of the prison walls he overpowered his lone guard, took his gun and fled in a stolen car. The most-wanted, most-recognized and most-despised man in Belgium was free for only three hours before he was apprehended, but the damage had been done. The minister of justice, the minister of the interior and the state police chief all resigned as a result. After seven years of investigation and preparation, Dutroux was brought to trial on 1 March 2004. But who else was involved?

Dutroux had always maintained that he occupied a lowly position in a hierarchy of paedophiles. He insisted that Jean-Michel Nihoul was the real person in charge.

Prosecutor Michel Bourlet acted on the theory that Dutroux had played a major role but had not been acting alone. There was, of course, Michel Lelièvre, who had been seen abducting Laetitia Delhez. Michelle Martin, who had divorced her husband in the months leading to the trial, was also thought to be guilty. After all, she had been in the Marcinelle house with several of the abducted girls. Bourlet believed that Jean-Michel Nihoul, too, was part of the paedophile ring, but there it stopped.

If conspiracy theorists were disappointed by the prosecutor's assessment of the situation, they were heartened three days into the trial when Dutroux claimed that he and Lelièvre had abducted An Marchal and Eefje Lambreks with the help of two

Laetitia Delhez (left) and Sabine Dardenne embrace after revisiting the cell where Dutroux imprisoned them

unidentified policemen. He added that he had not been involved in the death of either girl. Instead, they had been murdered by his co-defendants.

Throughout the trial, career criminal Dutroux concentrated his efforts on placing the blame upon others, while only accepting responsibility for the abductions and the sexual assaults. At times, he received unwitting support from other quarters. For example, Judge Jacques Langlois, who had spent years researching the crimes, testified that Dutroux was indeed innocent of the murders of Julie Lejeune and Melissa Russo.

However, he did not support Dutroux's story that Bernard Weinstein had been responsible. According to Judge Langlois, Michelle Martin had let the two girls starve to death while Dutroux was serving time in prison.

She had been asked by her then husband to feed the girls, but she had been fearful that they would attack her. How did the judge know this? Michelle herself had told him so.

Dutroux's boldness knew no bounds. On 20 April, during the second day of Sabine Dardenne's testimony, he implied that he had only abducted Laetitia Delhez so that she might have company.

'Is it not possible to silence this man?' the 20-year-old woman asked.

Dutroux was not put off by Sabine's hostility. He went on to claim that he had protected Sabine from a vast paedophile ring.

The verdicts

On 14 June 2004, what had become the most expensive and explosive court case in Belgian history finally came to an end. There had been three months of testimony, evidence and argument. The jury members – eight women and four men – were sequestered at an army barracks, where they were expected to reach their decision. They were required to consider around 400,000 pages of evidence and the testimonies of more than 500 witnesses, yet it took them less than three days to present the court with their initial verdicts.

Marc Dutroux was found guilty of murdering An Marchal, Eefje Lambreks and Bernie Weinstein, his one-time accomplice. He was also convicted of abducting and sexually assaulting all six of the girls.

Michel Lelièvre was found guilty of kidnapping, but not murder.

It would be some weeks before Jean-Michel Nihoul and Michelle Martin, Dutroux's ex-wife, would learn their fates.

Dutroux received a life sentence, with the added condition that he was to be 'put at the government's disposition'. In other words, he can never be released without the approval of the Belgian government.

The Monster's fate

After a few more weeks of deliberation, Michelle Martin was found guilty of murdering Julie Lejeune and Melissa Russo. She was sentenced to 30 years in jail. Michel Lelièvre was jailed for 25 years.

Throughout the investigations and the subsequent trial, the role of Jean-Michel Nihoul was never quite nailed down. Was he truly the mastermind of a paedophile ring, as Dutroux had alleged, or was it drugs and other criminal activities that had brought the two men together? Nihoul, the self-styled 'Monster of Brussels', claimed that he knew nothing of the kidnappings, rapes and murders committed by Dutroux. Ultimately, he was cleared of all of these offences, but he ended up serving five years in prison for drug offences and conspiracy.

Jean-Michel Nihoul, now a free man, lives in the small village of Zeebrugge on the Belgian coast. Michel Lelièvre and Michelle Martin will not be released until 2029 and 2034 respectively, and it is a safe assumption that Marc Dutroux will remain in prison for the rest of his life.

BRYAN AND DAVID FREEMAN
The Bloodied, God-fearing Home

Brothers Bryan and David Freeman may have been cut from the same cloth, but they bore no similarity to their parents. There were others like them, however, including their cousin Benny Birdwell. The trio were so often found together that they were often referred to as 'the Three Musketeers'. Desite the nickname, they had nothing in common with the heroes, Athos, Porthos and Aramis. And the setting of Alexandre Dumas' novel, 17th-century France, would not have suited them. No, the three boys would have felt most at home during the darkest, most violent days of Nazi Germany.

The Freeman boys weren't German, nor were they of German

descent. They had never been to Germany; indeed these boys from Allentown, Pennsylvania had never been outside the United States.

Bryan and David's father, Dennis, was a high school custodian and Brenda, their mother, was a housewife. Devout Jehovah's Witnesses, they were a modest couple who never wanted to draw attention to themselves. But life was bleak in the Freeman home in Allentown, particularly for a child, because Dennis and Brenda dedicated themselves to raising their children in accordance with the dictates of the Governing Body of Jehovah's Witnesses. Each December, Bryan and David looked on with envy as other children played with their new toys – Christmas was not celebrated in the Freeman household. Nor were birthdays. The two boys were not allowed to attend birthday parties and they could not look forward to their own. As he grew into adolescence, Bryan came to resent the fact that he had been deprived of many of the activities that were enjoyed by others of his age.

In 1991, Bryan and David left the church. That they did so together was not surprising. They were close allies in an increasingly hate-filled rebellion against their parents and everything they stood for. Bryan was 13 years old at the time and David was two years younger, yet their physical stature was that of much older boys. They were more than capable of carrying out the threats of violence they had made against their parents. Seven-year-old Erik, the third and final Freeman child, was also a target, for no other reason than the fact that he would not join his siblings in rejecting the church.

Forbidden fruit

Dennis and Brenda's constant attempts to bring their two eldest sons back as Jehovah's Witnesses only heightened their resentment.

The brothers embraced all things that had been forbidden. Born into a religion that condemned alcohol, the boys began to drink heavily. By the time they reached their mid-teens, Bryan and David began taunting their parents with talk of joining the military, a career path that went against the dictates of the church.

However, the military would never have considered the Freeman boys. It was nothing to do with their intelligence because Bryan had once been an honours student, and they were both fine physical specimens, standing over 6 ft (1.8m) tall and weighing over 200 lbs (90 kg). What would have prevented their admission into the army were the tattoos on their foreheads. 'SIEG HEIL' read David's, while his brother's said 'BERZERKER'. Bryan also had a swastika tattooed on the right side of his neck. The tattoos advertised the fact that both brothers were proud white supremacists. Bryan had been introduced to the movement in 1992, during a stay at a substance abuse treatment facility. David always followed Bryan in whatever he did, so he had been an eager convert to the cause.

Together with their older cousin, Benny Birdwell, they formed their own small group of skinheads which they named 'Berzerker' after the 9th-century Norse warriors of that name. They replaced the religion of their parents with the racist religious ideology of Christian Identity and they began attending services preached by Mark Thomas on a farm not far from Allentown.

By 1995 the situation in the Freeman household was deteriorating and the threats of violence were escalating, so the desperate Freeman parents were looking for help and support outside their church. Brenda turned to a group for parents of troubled children, the Pennsylvania Human Relations Commission and the B'Nai Brith's Anti-Defamation League. In early February 1995, Dennis and Brenda went through their sons' bedrooms and threw out all of the neo-Nazi books, pamphlets, posters and clothing.

But the purge only resulted in more threats of violence and death. In fact, David began to speak quite openly about how he was going to kill his mother. And the killing would not stop there, he said. He would steal a gun, kill a policeman who had once crossed him and then head south to Florida. His words were dismissed as crazy by some who heard them, while others took them seriously – but they were too frightened to speak up. Bryan also seemed to be getting angrier at the world. On 23 February, the former honours student threatened the high school principal and was suspended for five days. He would never return to school.

Dennis and Brenda might not have recognized the imminent danger posed by their eldest sons, but young Erik was more perceptive. When his aunt, Valerie Freeman, asked him how he was getting along with his brothers, the 11-year-old was quick to respond.

'You never know when you're going to die,' he said.

He then asked her to take care of his dog because he was afraid that his brothers would kill it.

If anything, Bryan and David had come to hate their younger brother even more than their parents because he would not rebel.

Instead, the 11-year-old boy was following a clearly defined path as a committed Jehovah's Witness.

Eerie silence

On the afternoon of 27 February 1995, Valerie arrived at the Freemans' home to find Dennis' truck in the driveway. It was a strange sight – he had never been known to leave work early.

From the left: David Freeman, Bryan Freeman and Nelson Birdwell III (Benny)

Things became more surreal when she tried the front door and found it locked. Dennis and Brenda were so trusting that they never barred their doors. She eventually gained access through the sliding glass doors at the side of the house. Inside there was an eerie silence. She called out but there was no response, so she walked farther into the house, heading towards the bedrooms. Thoroughly unnerved by this time, Valerie stopped outside Erik's closed door and knocked. Still no response. When she opened the door, Valerie saw the boy lying in the middle of a bed that was soaked in blood. He was obviously dead. Panicking, she rushed down the hall to the master bedroom, where she found Dennis bludgeoned to death on the bed. His throat had been slashed and his face had been struck with such force that his brain was exposed.

Valerie fled from the house in horror. Running to a neighbour, she phoned the police.

What the authorities found confirmed Valerie's fleeting visions. They also saw something that Valerie had missed – a bloodied aluminium baseball bat was leaning against a china cabinet in the dining room. Both Erik and Dennis were dead, but where was Brenda?

The police moved methodically through the house, ever aware that the killer or killers might still be present. After covering the ground floor, they turned their attention to the basement. And there they found their answer. Brenda lay dead on the cellar floor, with the hem of her nightgown around her waist. No search was needed to find the murder weapons. A knife lay next to her still body and there was a bloodied lead pipe on the stairs. It seemed that the killers had left a calling card – two swastikas had been drawn on the wall above Brenda's head. If that wasn't a big enough clue, Bryan and David were missing and so was the family car. As it turned out, Benny had also disappeared.

Capturing the three killers did not take much in the way of detective work. The brutal murders of Dennis, Brenda and Erik had hit the media. What is more, the boys' tattoos made it nearly impossible for them to blend in with the general population.

On the day after the murders were discovered, a truck driver reported that he had spotted the skinheads in Hubbard, Ohio, some 520 km (320 miles) west of Allentown. The three fugitives had spent the night at the Truck World Motor Inn. Though they had disappeared by the time the police arrived at the motel, they had left an important clue behind them. There was a record of a telephone call to the family farm of neo-Nazi Frank Hesse, which was situated just outside Michigan's Hope Township, about 180 km (110 miles) north-east of Grand Rapids.

Bryan, David and Benny were caught the day after the murder at the home of skinhead Frank Hesse. The neo-Nazi, who knew Bryan only because they had once met at a concert in Detroit, proved a welcoming host. But then, the boys didn't bother telling him that they were on the run after having committed three murders.

On 1 March, Hesse took Bryan, David and Benny ice fishing. As they returned to the farm they were surrounded by members of the FBI and a Michigan State Police SWAT team.

All of them were taken into custody, though Hesse was soon released when it became apparent that he had known nothing of the murders in Allentown.

When questioned, each boy offered a different account of the events that had surrounded the deaths of Dennis, Brenda and Erik.

David, the first to speak, related that he had gone out for fast food and a movie with Bryan and David on 26 February, the evening before the bodies were discovered. They had arrived home at 10.30 pm, half an hour before the curfew Brenda had imposed. She had been waiting up for them. Rather than face their mother, Bryan, David and their cousin had crawled in through a basement window.

Third time unlucky

Hearing the commotion, Brenda went downstairs and told her sons to go to bed. When they did not do so, she came down a second time and asked Benny to leave. He complied with her request, but then he crept back in through the basement window. Brenda went downstairs a third time, David said, but he was by then in his basement bedroom with Benny. He had heard Bryan and Brenda yelling at each other, but the noise had soon stopped.

David claimed that he had not witnessed his mother's murder. In fact, he did not know it had taken place until Bryan walked into his room. At that point Bryan told the other boys that they would be stabbed if they did not go upstairs and finish Dennis and Erik off. David admitted that he had killed his father and brother, but Benny had done nothing more than act as a witness to the slaughter. The 15-year-old rounded off his story by saying that he had dumped the knives he had used in the kitchen sink, placed the bat in the dining room, changed his clothes and left home for good.

Benny told a very different tale, though it began in much the same way. He spoke of fast food, a movie and Brenda's confrontation with her eldest son. In the middle of the yelling match, Bryan went into his basement bedroom and returned with a steak knife. He then grabbed his mother, put his hand over her mouth, and stabbed her in the back. Brenda collapsed on to the floor, but she managed to reach backwards and remove the knife. Bryan managed to wrestle it away from her and he stabbed her in the shoulder in the process. He then stuffed a pair of shorts into her mouth so that her screams would not alert Dennis and Erik.

Following Brenda's murder, Benny said that he had remained in the basement while the two brothers went on to kill Dennis and Erik. After Bryan and David had changed, all three of them got in the Freeman family car and began arguing about what to do. It was Bryan who suggested that they should hide out at Hesse's farm in Michigan. As they travelled west, the young killers considered returning to the house. Perhaps they could make the murders look like the result of a burglary that had gone wrong. That idea went out of the window when news reports about the killings started coming through.

Innocent bystander?

Benny insisted that he had nothing to do with the murders of Dennis, Brenda and Erik, despite his presence at the scene. He had joined the others in their escape because Bryan had told him not to 'puss out'. Benny's mother, who had driven to Michigan to see her son, believed his story. It mattered not one bit that his 'BERZERKER' tattoo matched Bryan's. Benny was 'a good boy'. In an effort to clear Benny's name, she told his story to a reporter from *The Midland Daily News*. Her efforts did him no favours.

What Benny's mother did not know was that the three boys had previously agreed on a plan of action. Working under the erroneous assumption that they could not be tried as adults, Bryan and David had agreed to take responsibility for the murders. That way Benny, an 18-year-old adult, would be saved from facing a murder trial. But when they read Benny's account of the murder in *The Midland Daily News*, the Freeman brothers felt betrayed. Their sense of injury was compounded by the news that under Pennsylvania law minors charged with homicide are eligible to be tried in an adult court.

Although Bryan had been steadfastly silent about the killings, he could not keep quiet any longer. Speaking for David as well as for himself, he said that the brothers would provide the authorities with a formal statement if their conditions were met – that is, that the prosecution would not seek the death penalty, the brothers would retain the right to a trial and they would be granted an interview with a journalist of their choosing.

The terms of the deal were accepted by prosecutor Robert Steinberg. On 6 March, the day on which their parents and their brother were buried, David and Bryan told the authorities what had really happened in the Freeman home.

David repeated the story he had told earlier, but with a significant difference. The 15-year-old maintained that he had not witnessed his mother's murder. After she had been killed he went upstairs with Benny, going first to where his father was sleeping. Benny struck the first blow, hitting Dennis in the face with a pickaxe handle. David then joined in the beating, using the aluminium baseball bat. Finally, Benny finished Dennis off by cutting his throat. By this point David could not take any more, so it was left to Benny to kill Erik.

Bloody shirt

Bryan told a nearly identical story, but he provided further details of Brenda's murder. He had stabbed her, much as his cousin had described, but Benny had not told the whole story. Bryan's cousin had clubbed Brenda with the pickaxe handle.

Steinberg was not satisfied with the two latest stories. Believing that both Bryan and David were lying, he cancelled the deal. After months of legal manoeuvring, the prosecution found evidence that contradicted Benny's story. Dennis Freeman's blood had been discovered on Benny's shirt, which discredited Benny's claim that he had stayed in the basement while the brothers had committed the murders upstairs.

On 7 December 1995, Bryan stood in court and admitted that he had killed his mother, thereby avoiding the death penalty. He was given a life sentence. A week later, David received an identical sentence after admitting that he had killed Dennis.

Only Benny would go to trial. On the first day of his trial, 26 March 1996, the defence revealed its strategy. With an IQ of 78 it was argued that Benny was borderline mentally retarded, so he was a follower, not a leader. He had blood on his shirt because he had walked into the bedroom as Dennis was being murdered.

On 26 April a jury decided that Benny had participated in the murder of Dennis Freeman. He was found guilty of murder in the first degree and was sentenced to life imprisonment without the possibility of parole.

JOSEF FRITZL
The Bunker Built for a Daughter

Josef Fritzl told conflicting stories about his mother Maria. In some, she was 'the best woman in the world', in others she had been a cold, brutal being – almost inhuman.

'She used to beat me, hit me until I was lying in a pool of blood on the floor,' he once claimed. 'I never had a kiss from her.'

Later on, Fritzl claimed, his mother did not mellow with age. Instead, her harsh nature stayed with her, even into old age. When Fritzl was a senior citizen himself, he revealed that Maria's last years were spent in a locked room with a bricked-up window. Fritzl told concerned neighbours that his mother had died, when in reality she had been his captive. In ordinary circumstances,

Fritzl's behaviour towards his mother would be shocking, but in the context of his other crimes the incident ranks as little more than a footnote.

Emergency call

The world knew nothing of Fritzl's crimes until the morning of Saturday 19 April 2008, when he telephoned for an ambulance. Seventeen-year-old Kerstin Fritzl was seriously ill at his home, number 40 Ybbsstrasse in the Austrian town of Amstetten.

The ambulance attendants were puzzled by the condition of their unconscious patient. Her symptoms were like nothing they had ever encountered. Deathly pale and missing many of her teeth, Kerstin was close to death. She was transported immediately to the local hospital. A few hours later, Josef Fritzl turned up. Describing himself as her grandfather, he presented a letter from Kerstin's mother, Elisabeth.

> 'Please help her. Kerstin is very scared of strangers. She has never been in a hospital before. I've asked my father for help because he is the only person she knows.'

Josef Fritzl explained Elisabeth had run off to join a religious cult many years before, leaving the child with him. The police were called in as Kerstin lay close to death and a team of investigators began a search for Elisabeth Fritzl. The authorities wanted to question the mother about what they thought might be criminal neglect. Enquiries were made all over Austria and all sorts of databases were checked, yet nothing could be found on Elisabeth that was not at least a few decades old.

Televised appeal

At the end of Kerstin's second day in hospital, the doctors made a televised appeal. They were struggling to diagnose Kerstin's condition and they thought that her mother might be able to help them. When Elisabeth failed to contact the hospital the police showed up at 40 Ybbsstrasse. They wanted to take DNA samples from the Fritzls. Josef's wife Rosemarie provided a sample, as did the other children that Elisabeth had previously abandoned. However, Josef himself was far too busy to give the authorities even a few minutes of his time.

One week after Kerstin had been taken to hospital, Rosemarie was surprised to see Elisabeth in her house. Her daughter had been away for nearly 24 years. Elisabeth was accompanied by two children, Stefan and Felix. Rosemarie had not been aware of their existence. Josef explained that their daughter had heard the doctors' appeals and had left the cult she had been with, so that she could see her seriously ill daughter.

When Elisabeth visited the hospital, the police were waiting. They wanted to know where the young woman had been during the previous two decades, and how it was that she had abandoned her children. Elisabeth was taken to the police station, where she was questioned for hours. As midnight approached, Elisabeth revealed that she had not joined a cult and she had not abandoned her children. Instead, she had been imprisoned by her father in the cellar at 40 Ybbsstrasse.

Having broken her silence, Elisabeth told the police that she would reveal everything about the last 24 years of her life on condition that she never had to see her father again.

After the stunned investigators had acceded to her wishes,

Elisabeth began a two-hour monologue in which she described in considerable detail the ordeal she had endured.

She told the police that her father had lured her into the cellar on 29 August 1984, where she had been sedated with ether and placed in a hidden bunker.

It seemed that the foundations of number 40 Ybbsstrasse were something of a maze. The oldest part of the house dated back to 1890 and numerous modifications had been made in the years that followed, including a 1978 addition that had been constructed by a builder.

For reasons of secrecy, however, Fritzl had built the bunker himself. It could only be reached by going down the cellar stairs, passing through a number of rooms and unlocking a series of eight doors. The final door was hidden behind a large shelving unit.

The bunker itself consisted of a kitchen, a bathroom, a living area and two bedrooms. There was no source of natural light, and the air was stale and stagnant. The ceiling was very low – it was less than 2 m (6 ft) high at best. It had not been difficult for Fritzl to construct the bunker. As an electrical engineer, he had always been good with his hands.

Good provider

Born in Amstetten on 9 April 1935, Fritzl had been raised alone by his mother after his father had deserted his small family. Josef Fritzl Snr went on to fight as a Nazi stormtrooper and was killed during the Second World War. The younger Josef had been a good student with a notable aptitude for technical matters. He had just begun his career with a Linz steel company when he married

17-year-old Rosemarie at the age of 21. The couple had two sons and five daughters together, including the beautiful Elisabeth.

Fritzl was a very good provider, but he was also an unpleasant husband and father. In 1967 he was sentenced to 18 months in prison after having confessed to the rape of a 24-year-old woman. After his release he was employed by a construction firm and later on he travelled throughout Austria as a technical equipment salesman. Until April 2008, the electrical engineer had no further brushes with the law. That is not to say that he led an exemplary life. Among his neighbours he had a reputation as an unfriendly man, one who kept himself to himself and his family away from others. There was talk that he was very firm with his children and that absolute obedience was expected.

No matter how much Fritzl's neighbours gossiped about him, none of them had the faintest conception of what was taking place in his household. In 1977, Fritzl began sexually abusing Elisabeth. She was 11 years old at the time. Although she told no one, not even her close friend Christa Woldrich, it is easy to imagine what a devastating effect it must have had on her.

'I did get the impression that she felt more comfortable at school than at home,' Woldrich told one reporter. 'Sometimes she went quiet when it was time to go home again.'

In January 1983, Elisabeth ran away from home, ending up in Vienna. She was then 16 years old. Even though she tried her best to hide, she only managed to remain free for three weeks before the police found her and returned her to her parents. The authorities calculate that Fritzl was well into the construction of the bunker at this point. Eighteen months after the police had brought the girl back to number 40 Ybbsstrasse, Elisabeth's incarceration began.

Fritzl appeared to be very open about what had happened to his 18-year-old daughter.

He told everyone that she had been a drug-taking problem child who had gone off to join a religious cult. But there was no cult, of course. Fritzl backed up his story by forcing Elisabeth to write a letter in which she told everyone not to search for her because she was now happy.

Elisabeth was alone in the bunker until the birth of her first child. Her only visitor was her father, who would arrive every few days to bring her food. He would then rape her. The nightmare became greater still during Elisabeth's fourth year underground when she became pregnant for the first time, suffering a miscarriage. Elisabeth's second pregnancy led to the birth of Kerstin and Stefan arrived in the following year. There would be seven children in all, including Michael, who died when he was three days old. While Kerstin, Stefan and Felix, the youngest, lived in captivity, Fritzl arranged for the others to be taken care of by Rosemarie.

It had been difficult to explain the babies away. After all, Rosemarie knew nothing of the bunker. Like everyone else, she believed the troubled Elisabeth had achieved some sort of happiness as a member of a fictitious cult. However, Fritzl had already laid the groundwork by portraying Elisabeth as an unstable and irresponsible daughter. All that remained was to smuggle the babies upstairs in the middle of the night and then leave them on the front doorstep with a note from Elisabeth.

In May 1993, 9-month-old Lisa became the first of the grandchildren who would be cared for by Rosemarie. When Monika appeared in the following year, the press took note. 'What kind of mother would do such a thing?' asked one newspaper.

After having raised seven of her own children, the neighbours took pity on Rosemarie. However, the senior citizen made no complaints and she proved to be devoted to her grandchildren. All three did well at school and they seemed happy and healthy, despite their incestuous background. Even the unfriendly Fritzl received a certain amount of respect and admiration for helping to raise three young children during the years in which one might rightly expect to take things easy.

For the children in the bunker, life could not have been more different. Kerstin, Stefan and Felix knew they had siblings living in the house above their heads. Indeed, Kerstin and Stefan could remember the babies being taken away. To add insult to injury, Josef would bring videos that showed Lisa, Monika and Alexander enjoying a lifestyle that was vastly superior to their own.

Despite her suffering, Elisabeth did her best to provide Kerstin, Stefan and Felix with some semblance of a normal upbringing. She gave them regular lessons, in which they learned reading, writing and mathematics. All of the children, whether they were raised in the bunker by Elisabeth or upstairs by Rosemarie, ended up being intelligent, articulate and polite.

In the bunker

Fritzl has never explained why he took Lisa, Monika and Alexander upstairs, while keeping their siblings captive below. One possible explanation might have been lack of space. With a total area of around 35 square metres (380 square feet) the bunker was becoming increasingly cramped, particularly when the children grew bigger.

After the birth of Monika in 1993, Fritzl alleviated the

problem somewhat by expanding the size of the bunker to 55 square metres (600 square feet).

On 27 April 2008, nine days after Fritzl had telephoned for an ambulance, a number of police officers arrived at the house of Josef and Rosemarie Fritzl. Josef Fritzl was taken into custody while Rosemarie and her grandchildren were taken to a psychiatric hospital, where they were reunited with Elisabeth.

On the day after his arrest, Fritzl confessed to keeping Elisabeth captive and fathering her children. He defended his actions by claiming that the sex had been consensual and that Elisabeth's incarceration had been necessary in order to rescue her from 'persons of questionable moral standards'. Elisabeth

A police van stands outside the house in Amstetten as officers begin to untangle Fritzl's web of incest

had refused to obey his rules ever since she had entered puberty, he said.

As Fritzl awaited trial for his crimes he became more and more enraged by the media coverage. Eventually, the electrical engineer released a letter through his lawyer in which he spoke of the kindness he had shown his family. Fritzl pointed out that he could have killed them, but chose not to.

On 16 March 2009, the first day of his trial, Fritzl was charged with rape, incest, kidnapping, false imprisonment, slavery, grievous assault and the murder of baby Michael. He pleaded guilty to all of the charges with the exception of grievous assault and murder.

In keeping with the agreement she struck with the police on the day she finally emerged from the bunker, Elisabeth did not appear in court. Instead, the 42-year-old woman's testimony was presented in the form of an 11-hour video recording. The prosecution later revealed that Elisabeth had been watching the proceedings from the visitors' gallery. She had been heavily disguised to avoid being recognized.

The news caused Fritzl to break down. He changed his plea to guilty on all charges, thereby ending the court case. That same day he was sentenced to life imprisonment, with no possibility of parole for 15 years.

JOHN WAYNE GACY
The Cemetry in the Crawl Space

T hings were looking desperate for John Wayne Gacy in the spring of 1992. Thirteen years had passed since he had been convicted of 33 counts of murder and he had spent 13 long years on Death Row. Now, with his avenues of appeal all but exhausted, he turned to the public forum in an effort to win a new trial. He gave a prison interview in which he argued his innocence.

'If people don't want to know the truth and the honesty of it, if they want to be convinced or brainwashed into what they believe, then fine, then go ahead and kill me,' said the condemned man.

Then, misquoting *Romans 12:19*, he threatened his listeners. '"Vengeance is mine, saith the Lord" because you will have executed somebody who didn't commit the crime.'

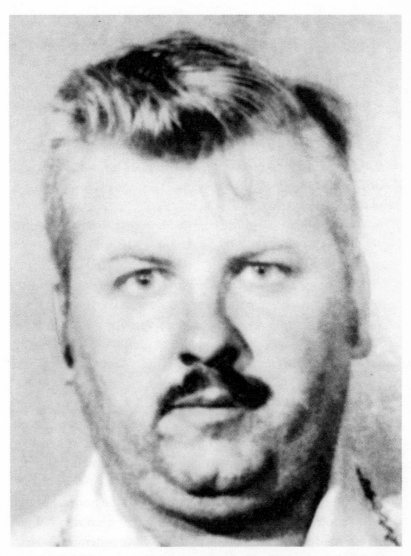

John Wayne Gacy was a pillar of his community and entertained audiences as Pogo the Clown, but lurking beneath this jolly exterior was something more sinister

Bullied and beaten

Gacy was born in Chicago on St Patrick's Day, 1942. Though he was an eldest son, and was named after his father, he did not have a place of privilege within the household. Gacy Snr, an alcoholic machinist, would bully and beat him – as he would the rest of the family. And yet, Gacy practically worshipped his father. He strove to prove himself worthy of the old man's affections, but earned neither his love nor his approval. Though there was nothing particularly effeminate about Gacy, his father would call him a 'sissy' and a 'Mama's boy'.

Apart from his relationship with his father, Gacy had other problems. As a 9-year-old, he was molested by a friend of the family and two years later a child's swing hit his forehead, causing a blood clot to develop in his brain. The resulting blackouts only brought more ridicule from Gacy Snr, who said his son was merely seeking attention. As Gacy matured, his condition worsened, until it was diagnosed and treated with drugs. In the following year he was hospitalized with a heart ailment, the cause of which remained a mystery.

Despite all of these obstacles and setbacks, the young Gacy was a hardworking lad who had several after-school jobs. School itself proved more of a challenge, because he was a middling student with no real passion for learning. He moved from one high school to another before dropping out in his senior year.

By the age of 20, Gacy had begun standing up to his father. One confrontation between the two resulted in his leaving home. Thinking the city flush with well-paid, interesting jobs, Gacy moved to Las Vegas. But he had made a big mistake. He spent the next three months working as a funeral home janitor, all the while trying to earn enough money for a ticket back to Chicago. The bitter experience taught Gacy the value of education. He enrolled in Northwestern Business College, where he proved himself to be a good student. After he graduated he soon found employment with the Nunn-Bush Shoe Company, who transferred him to Springfield, Illinois, the state capital.

An energetic 22-year-old salesman, Gacy was climbing the ranks not only at the Nunn-Bush Shoe Company, but in the community as a whole. He volunteered for a number of local organizations, including the Jaycees (a US youth service organization) who would name him 'Man of the Year'. Gacy appeared to be just as successful in his private life. In 1964, he married a pretty co-worker named Marlynn Myers. Shortly afterwards, the newlyweds left their place of employment and moved west to the bride's home town of Waterloo, Iowa. Once there, Gacy managed three fried chicken outlets owned by Marlynn's father.

Cheating on his wife

Marriage and the move to Waterloo appear to have brought about a change in Gacy. Not long after arriving in the small city, he began cheating on his wife with both men and women. In 1967, the year that he was named 'outstanding vice-president' by the Jaycees, Gacy began having sex with the teenage male employees of the Kentucky Fried Chicken restaurants. He encouraged the youths to drink and he often gave them money to perform.

Gacy's behaviour became increasingly aberrant. Finally, in May 1968 he was arrested for raping one of his male employees. The victim, 16-year-old Mark Miller, had told the police that he had been tied up and sodomized during a visit to the Gacy home in the previous year. Gacy sought to defend himself by accusing the Jaycees of framing him.

Just before his court appearance, Gacy hired Dwight Anderson to physically assault Miller, in the hope that it would discourage the teenager from giving his testimony. However, it was Anderson who suffered the worst in the confrontation, coming away with a broken nose. Gacy was arrested again after Anderson confessed he had been given $310 to carry out the beating.

On 3 December 1968, Gacy was handed a ten-year sentence for sodomy. That same day, Marlynn filed for divorce. He never saw his wife or the two children again. Faced with the inevitable, Gacy worked hard to become a model prisoner, even going so far as to join the prison Jaycees. Among Gacy's projects was the construction of a miniature golf course for his fellow inmates.

On 18 June 1970, after having served just over 18 months of his sentence, he was released on parole. With no home to go to, Gacy returned to Chicago, where he lived with his now-widowed mother.

Sexual assault

The former fast food restaurant manager got a job as a short order cook and he seems to have lived a quiet life for at least a few months. However, on 12 February 1971 he was charged with sexual assault, after a teenage boy complained that Gacy had tried to force him to have sex in his car. The charges were dismissed when the accuser failed to show up in court. It was one of two lucky breaks that came Gacy's way.

The other one was the fact that the Iowa Board of Parole never learned of the accusation. Several months later, Gacy's mother gave him the money for a down payment on a bungalow at

8213 West Summerdale Avenue in the Norwood Park Township, which bordered the city of Chicago.

Once settled, the community-minded Gacy again joined a number of volunteer organizations. The 29-year-old also reconnected with an old high school flame named Carol Hoff.

A divorcée with two daughters, Carol knew that her old beau had spent time in prison, but she strongly believed that he had emerged a better man. On 1 June 1972, she married Gacy and then moved into the West Summerdale Avenue bungalow with her daughters. Three weeks later, unbeknownst to his new bride, Gacy was arrested after using a fake sheriff's badge to lure a young man into his car and trying to force him to have sex. The charges were dropped after Gacy's accuser was caught attempting to blackmail him.

To neighbours, the new couple seemed meant for each other. Gacy's wife neither knew nor suspected that anything was amiss and she joined enthusiastically in Gacy's community activities. The pair organized and hosted several street parties, including one event that was attended by over 300 guests. Carol watched delightedly as her husband toured the children's wards in hospitals, dressed in a clown costume of his own design.

In 1972, Gacy quit his job as a cook to start his own painting and decorating business. It was a successful enterprise from the beginning and within six years it was grossing $200,000 per annum. When Gacy needed employees, he invariably turned to teenage boys, particularly those who were blond and muscular. Because he was in the decorating business and was surrounded by attractive young men, people started to whisper that Gacy was gay.

As his marriage to Carol was entering its fourth year, Gacy told her that he was bisexual. With this news, he began staying out at night, using the excuse that he was working late. From there he moved on to entertaining teenage boys in the garage. Carol found it difficult to stop her daughters from seeing the gay pornography that her husband was leaving about the house. Unsurprisingly, the couple divorced in March 1976.

Despite his criminal record and the rumours about his relations with teenage boys, Gacy began taking steps towards a career in politics. He did volunteer work for the Democratic Party, slowly rising through the ranks. On one occasion he even met First Lady Rosalynn Carter at a special event.

A photograph showed Gacy wearing a distinctive pin, a sign that he had received special security clearance. The episode became a huge embarrassment to the Secret Service seven months later, when Gacy's real character was exposed.

Handcuffs, various driving licences, a 1975 high school class ring and a receipt from a pharmacy – these are just a few of the items that the police uncovered when they began searching the West Summerdale Avenue bungalow on 13 December 1978. They were looking for clues relating to the previous day's disappearance of a 15-year-old boy named Robert Piest. The receipt was of particular interest because it came from the pharmacy at which Robert worked – and it had been printed at almost the exact time that he had disappeared. The last person to see Robert had been his mother. She had arrived at the store to pick up her son but he had waved her off, telling her that he wanted to speak to a local contractor about getting a new job.

When Robert failed to return home, his mother contacted the police. Fortunately, she had remembered the name that was written on the side of Gacy's truck. Several hours later, a police officer was at Gacy's front door. Gacy told the man that he was unable to leave the house because there had been a death in the family and he had telephone calls to make. He later appeared at the police station, where he gave a statement in which he denied ever speaking to Robert. Gacy did himself no favours when he went back to the police station at 3.30 in the morning, covered in mud. He explained that he had just been in a motor accident. After that, he simply repeated the claims he had made hours earlier.

A search warrant was issued after the police ran a background check that revealed Gacy's sodomy conviction. The pharmacy receipt was just one of hundreds of items to be carted away from 8213 West Summerdale Avenue. Many of the objects belonged to Piest and the other young males that had gone missing in the Chicago area.

It was damning evidence, but the find was soon eclipsed by the 27 bodies that police discovered in the crawl space that served as the foundation of the house.

Gacy had been in custody for a week before he confessed to killing the boys and men whose remains had been found beneath his house. He thought the total was 30, but he had lost count. He had certainly killed more than 27 people. Although the crawl space had made a good-sized burial ground, it had proved too small to accommodate all of Gacy's victims.

When he ran out of space, he had begun dumping corpses in the Des Plaines River. The vast majority of the murders had taken place in Gacy's bungalow, beginning with that of 15-year-old Timothy Jack McCoy. This had taken place on 3 January 1974, less than 18 months after Gacy had been released from prison. According to Gacy, the boy's death was the tragic result of a misunderstanding.

On the previous day he had picked up McCoy at Chicago's

Greyhound bus terminal. After a day spent sightseeing, the boy had ended up spending the night at the West Summerdale Avenue bungalow. Gacy claimed that when McCoy had prepared breakfast he had innocently walked into the bedroom carrying a kitchen knife. Thinking he was about to be attacked, Gacy grabbed the knife and stabbed the boy to death. He only realized his mistake when he saw the breakfast that McCoy had prepared.

Cold, calculated killing

The second murder was completely calculated. While his wife and stepdaughters were away visiting relatives in July 1975, he had lured one of his disgruntled employees, 17-year-old John Butkovitch, to his home. After handcuffing the boy, Gacy sat on his chest for a while before strangling him.

After Carol and his stepdaughters moved out, Gacy had the house to himself and the rate of killing accelerated. He would entrap his victims by using what he said were trick handcuffs. Once at his mercy, each of them would be chloroformed and raped. The torture and sexual abuse would last for hours, invariably ending in death from strangulation or asphyxiation.

Sex toys

A glimpse into Gacy's routine was provided by Jeffrey Ringall, one of the few young men to survive his visit to Gacy's home. He first encountered Gacy while walking through New Town, an area of Chicago known for its bars and nightclubs.

After a short conversation, the older man invited Ringall to smoke some marijuana in his car. Ringall was enjoying the first joint when Gacy shoved a chloroform-doused cloth in his face. At that point he drifted in and out of consciousness. When he came round, Ringall found himself handcuffed in the West Summerdale Avenue bungalow. Gacy stood naked in front of him while he showed off his large collection of sex toys. Ringall was raped, tortured and drugged. On the next morning he awoke fully clothed in Chicago's Lincoln Park.

Fortunately for Ringall, Gacy realized that it would be nearly impossible for the young man to identify him or tell the authorities where he had been held captive. But Gacy's actions still betrayed a certain recklessness. While it was true that he preyed primarily on male prostitutes and teenage runaways, Gacy had been bold enough to murder several of his employees. John Butkovitch had been just one of four boys who had disappeared while working for Gacy's decorating company, yet the local authorities had failed to spot a link.

At his trial on 6 February 1980, Gacy retracted the confession he had made 15 months earlier. Pleading not guilty by reason of insanity, he joked that he was guilty of nothing more than 'running a cemetery without a licence'. Gacy's lawyer claimed that his client suffered from multiple personality disorder. The murders, he argued, had not been committed by John Wayne Gacy but by an alter ego named Jack.

Despite the best efforts of his defence lawyers, on 13 March Gacy was found guilty of 33 murders and was sentenced to death. Nine of the boys he had murdered were never identified. He was then transferred to the maximum security Menard Correctional Center, where he sat for 14 years on Death Row. Maintaining his innocence to the end, he was executed on 10 May 1994.

What were the final words of the man who had quoted biblical scriptures in his defence?

'Kiss my ass.'

ED GEIN
A Farmhouse Full
of Body Parts

With a population of roughly 900 souls, the village of Plainfield is not much larger than when Gein knew it. Located in central Wisconsin, it is the sort of community where everyone seems to know pretty well everyone else. The good folks of Plainfield knew 51-year-old Ed Gein, for example, even though he lived alone in an isolated farmhouse outside the village. One elderly gentleman described Ed as 'a nice man just like anybody else', but then he added: 'The only difference I'd say in the man, he seems to be a little odd.'

But Ed was not as well known as Bernice Worden. As the proprietor of the village's only hardware store, one of just a handful of businesses in Plainfield, Bernice was a presence in the community. So when she failed to open up Worden's Hardware

Ed Gein seemed like a nice guy, but there was always something a little strange about him

and Implement Store one morning, people in Plainfield started to talk. That day, 16 November 1957, marked the beginning of the deerhunting season. Could it be that Bernice had decided to take the day off, thinking that business would be slow? It was not like her.

In the late afternoon, Bernice's son came back from the hunt. After he had opened up the store he found blood on the floor. He quickly called the police. When they arrived, he had no hesitation in pointing to Ed Gein as a possible suspect. Why not?

Ed was recognized as a peculiar man. He was pleasant enough but he did not quite fit in. Just recently he had asked Bernice whether she would like to go roller-skating with him. It was an odd invitation to come from a life-long bachelor, particularly one who had always seemed so uncomfortable around women.

Two hours after Bernice had been reported missing, two sheriff's deputies drove out to Ed's farm. It was dark at this point and the farmhouse seemed darker still. When their loud knocking brought no response, the two men decided to investigate the woodshed. There they discovered Bernice's remains, hanging upside-down from the rafters. She had been decapitated and gutted, much like a deer that had just been killed in that day's hunt.

The law caught up with Gein that same night, just as he had finished dinner at the home of the town's grocer. He was arrested and taken to the Wautoma County jailhouse. As he settled into his cell, the police carried on searching the woodshed, before moving on to his home. It was filthy and it was filled with twelve years' worth of rubbish. But there was more. Mixed in with the old newspapers, rags and empty tin cans were objects that had been crafted from human bodies. These included a string of nipples that had been cut from various breasts, a shade pull that had been made from a woman's lips and bowls that were actually the tops of skulls. In the living room was a lampshade of stretched human skin, the same 'material' that had been used to upholster the chairs.

There were decorations, too. Ed had crafted nine facemasks by flaying the skin from the heads of his victims and then stuffing the resulting face shapes with paper. After that he had hung them on the wall. He had not done this with everyone, though.

One officer found a brown paper grocery bag that contained the severed head of Mary Hogan, a local bar owner who had vanished three years earlier.

Moving through the house, the police came across a room that had been boarded up.

The men braced themselves for a shock. What new horrors would they have to face?

Mother complex

When the door was finally opened the jittery police officers stumbled into a well-ordered, tidy room, in which nothing was out of place. It had belonged to Ed's mother, Augusta Gein, who had died 12 years earlier. The worst thing one could say about the bedroom was that it was dusty. In all likelihood, Ed had not been in the room since the time of his mother's death. Ed had really loved his mother, perhaps obsessively. She brought him into the world on 27 August 1906, in La Crosse County, Wisconsin and she stayed close to him until the day she died.

Ed's fondness for her was in sharp contrast to his feelings for George, his grocer father. Abusive and alcoholic, he had also been a control freak. George's move to the large house on the outskirts of tiny Plainfield, with its 200-acre farm, had everything to do with his desire to hold sway over Ed and his elder brother Henry.

However, Augusta had also been very much in favour of the move. She did not like La Crosse – indeed, she considered it to be the Sodom and Gomorrah of Wisconsin. Augusta was a devout woman, a dour Lutheran who would never entertain so much as a thought about leaving her miserable marriage. To Augusta, divorce was a mortal sin – just like her husband's drinking. She would spend each afternoon with her boys, reading passages from the Old Testament. From an early age, Ed and Henry were taught that women were by and large nothing but whores.

Ed's only break from life in the farmhouse came when he attended school in Plainfield. However, his slight build and his effeminate manner encouraged bullies. And he made no friends because Augusta forbade it.

After he left school at the age of 14, Ed rarely left the farm. For the next 20 years he saw almost no one except his mother, his father and his brother. In 1940, when Ed was 34 years old, George was felled by a heart attack. As no one on the farm had much of a head for figures, George's death resulted in a reduction in the family income. For the first time, the Gein boys looked to make money in town. Both developed reputations as dependable handymen and Ed even spent his evenings babysitting young children.

'He was a hard worker,' said one neighbour of Ed. 'When you paid him a dollar you got a dollar-and-a-half's worth of work out of him. He didn't slack off, he wouldn't screw anything up.'

In 1944 the family suffered another tragedy when Henry was killed fighting a brushfire. It was a curious death, unlike anything the investigators had ever seen. Ed's brother had been found bruised and beaten in the middle of an area that had been untouched by the flames. Nevertheless, the county coroner determined the cause of death as asphyxiation. For 17 months Ed lived alone with Augusta on the Gein farm, until she too died, after having suffered several strokes.

Now totally alone, Ed longed for companionship. However, his mother had instilled a distrust of others in him, as well as a fear of human contact. But with the repressive and stern Augusta

The kitchen of the farmhouse – in a nearby shed was the body of Bernice Worden dressed out like a freshly killed deer

gone, his pent-up thoughts and desires were let loose, until his bloody progress was brought to a halt on that cold, dark November day in 1957.

Sitting alone in his cell at the Wautoma County jailhouse, Ed knew that his house was being searched. He was all too aware of the secrets it would reveal and yet he said nothing. It was not until the police accused him of killing Bernice that he began to speak.

Well, not quite.

Ed would not speak until he had been given a slice of apple pie with a piece of cheddar cheese on top of it. After he had gobbled it down, he became quite talkative.

He told the investigators that almost all of his arts and crafts projects had been made possible by exhuming recently-deceased corpses from the local cemeteries. He obtained his information about future burials by reading the obituaries in the local newspapers. On the following evening he would then dig up the fresh grave and remove the body.

Ed's description of his ghoulish activities might have reflected something of his loneliness, but it did not explain the string of nipples or the lampshade made from human skin.

Even more bizarre, the police had discovered a gruesome artefact that they referred to as 'the mammary vest'. Ed had attached straps to the upper torso of a woman, so that it could be worn. He had also made leggings from the skin of a woman's legs.

Despite all the evidence, he would only confess to the murders of Bernice Worden and Mary Hogan, the first victims the police were able to identify.

Ed had known Mary through Hank's Place, the rough watering hole she ran in Pine Grove, a small town roughly 13 km (seven miles) from his home.

Mary was just the sort of woman Augusta had always warned her sons about. She drank, she swore and she told dirty stories. In short, Mary was a good-time gal. Augusta would have considered her a whore amongst whores.

It is likely that Ed killed Mary on 8 December 1954. That afternoon a local farmer entered the tavern to find it deserted. There was money strewn about the floor, some of it soaking in a pool of blood.

The police officers who investigated Mary's disappearance never thought to question Ed. And yet Ed told people that Mary was at his farm.

One Plainfield resident recalled Ed's blunt admission. 'Somebody said, "Well, I wonder where Mary Hogan is?" "Oh," he said, "she's over by my place. I got her over there."

And everybody said, "Ah, Eddie, you got her. Yeah, we know Eddie."'

It was not the only time Ed had made that same confession. He often spoke about Mary. 'She's not missing. She's down at the house now,' he once said.

It was too much to imagine that the quiet, reclusive, hardworking bachelor, the man who was a trusted babysitter, might be the killer.

By the next afternoon, less than a day after Bernice's son had seen his mother's blood on her hardware store floor, Ed had put Plainfield on the map.

Though the details were still sketchy, and there was so much more to learn, news of his crimes had made him nationally known.

It seemed that each day marked the discovery of another nightmarish object on the Gein farm. On 16 January 1958, Ed Gein was charged with one count of first-degree murder, but his defence lawyers entered a plea of not guilty by reason of insanity.

The doctors who took the stand testified that he suffered from schizophrenia and was prone to hallucinations. Ed had told them that he believed himself to be an instrument of God, blessed with the ability to raise the dead. That same day, Ed was declared legally insane. He would not be tried for the murders of Bernice and Mary. He was committed to the Central State Hospital for the Criminally Insane in Waupun. He had been there for just over two months when the Gein farmhouse and all it contained was consumed by a mysterious fire.

Ed was not troubled by the news.

'Just as well,' he said.

Ed was not troubled by much, in fact. Quiet, polite and

obedient, he was content to spend his days reading the newspaper in the hospital's dayroom. It was only during a full moon that he displayed any unusual behaviour. On those evenings he would ramble on about women and what he would like to do to them.

Still deranged

In 1968, his doctors decided that he was competent enough to be tried for Bernice Worden's murder. A decade had passed since Ed had last been seen in public. The man who entered the courtroom looked remarkably different. Now 62 years old, Ed was a little heavier. His hair, which had been dark brown, had turned white.

At the end of his trial, which lasted nine days, he was declared guilty. The verdict meant precisely nothing – Ed was returned to the hospital, where he lived out his remaining days.

Ed Gein died on 26 July 1984 at the age of 77. He had succumbed to respiratory heart failure following cancer.

Though Ed's name still ranks high in the hall of infamy, it has been eclipsed by the fictional characters that his exploits have inspired. The first of these creations was Norman Bates, the protagonist of Robert Bloch's 1959 novel *Psycho*, whose relationship with his mother mirrors that of Ed and Augusta.

Thirteen years after Alfred Hitchcock adapted Bloch's nightmarish novel for the cinema, Ed was the model for Leatherface, who appears in the 1974 cult classic *The Texas Chainsaw Massacre*. Other cinematic characters owed their existence to Ed, the most notable being Buffalo Bill, who tries to make a 'woman suit' out of real skin in *The Silence of the Lambs*.

FRITZ HAARMANN
The Apartment Slaughterhouse

Fritz Haarmann's final wish was to be given a public execution in the market place of his home town of Hanover. He dreamed of being buried under a tombstone which would bear the inscription 'Here Lies Mass-Murderer Haarmann' and he wanted a memorial wreath to be laid every year on his birthday. In the end, the man who was known as the Butcher of Hanover was indeed executed, though the grisly event, death by decapitation, took place within the walls of Hanover Prison – hidden from the public gaze. There would be no tombstone and the exact location of the better part of his remains is unknown. However, we do know that his head is kept in the Faculty of Medicine at the University of Göttingen. Although it has been studied for more than eight decades, it has yet to give up any secrets, yet there is something appropriate in the fact that Haarmann's head continues to be housed separately from the rest of his body. After all, it was the discovery of a skull that finally brought the bloody trail of Germany's most prolific serial killer to an end.

Haarmann didn't look like he could kill. Born in 1879, the sixth child of an unhappy, mismatched couple, from an early age he gravitated towards the feminine. No one would have expected him to become a killer because he displayed feminine tendencies from an early age. While his brothers played sports, young Fritz liked nothing more than to stay at home with his sister's dolls. Encouraged by his mother, he spoke like a girl, moved like a girl and spent much of his time baking and cooking. When he was 16 years old his father enrolled him in a military academy, perhaps in an effort to make a man of him. At first he thrived on the discipline and order, but then he fell victim to seizures and other manifestations of ill health. Haarmann left the school so that he could take a job with his father... and then the real trouble began.

He was caught molesting young children, even though he had once been a victim himself. As a result, he was committed to an asylum at the age of 18, an experience that would scar him for life. Indeed, he once declared that he preferred hanging to treatment in 'the loony bin'. When he saw an opportunity for escape he took it. He then lived in Switzerland for a time, before returning to Hanover.

Now 20 years old, the once unstable child molester seemed prepared to live a life of quiet domesticity. He worked, married and fathered a child. However, Haarmann abandoned his wife for the army before the baby was born. It was an odd and unexpected move, one that could only be explained by his attraction to military order. But history would repeat itself. As before, he initially flourished under military training only to suffer a physical and mental breakdown. As 1901 drew to an end, Haarmann, now 22 years old, was discharged from the army. He did not return to his wife, who had since given birth. Instead he turned his back on all of his obligations, as well as anything else that might have offered him stability.

Haarmann became a petty crook, making frequent trips to prison for fraud, burglary and smuggling. Added to his list of crimes were numerous sexual offences, though these rarely resulted in incarceration. There was one notable exception, when a police detective entered Haarmann's cramped apartment on 25 September 1918 and found him in bed with a young boy. Haarmann was sentenced to nine months' imprisonment as a result, but would most certainly have received more had the room been searched. Behind the stove the child molester had stuffed the head of Friedel Rothe, a 17-year-old runaway he had murdered just days before. It was a lucky break.

The police visit had been part of an effort to locate Rothe, but discovering Haarmann in the act of molesting a second boy had thrown them off the scent. Incredibly, they never got around to searching the room.

Gay lover

Haarmann had plenty of time to get rid of Rothe's head because 18 months elapsed before he began serving his sentence. By the time he entered prison the 40-year-old killer was involved with yet another teenage runaway, but this particular boy, the handsome Hans Grans, was not killed like the others. Instead, he became Haarmann's homosexual lover.

The couple reunited on Christmas Day 1920, when Haarmann was released from prison. In tolerant Weimar Germany, the sight of a homosexual couple with an age disparity brought little attention. Indeed, Haarmann and Grans attracted more notice because of their philanthropy. Their generosity came not in the form of money – though Haarmann was making a good living through burglary and his work as a police informant – but in distributing old clothing to the needy.

The couple also ran a stall opposite the Hanover train station, where they sold used jackets, trousers and shirts. These activities were very risky because some of the clothing was stolen and the remainder came from the men and boys that Haarmann had killed.

After he had murdered Friedel Rothe, Haarmann claimed that he did not kill again for four and a half years. He took the life of his second victim, 17-year-old Fritz Franke, on 12 February 1923. The scene of the crime was the modest one-room Neuestrasse apartment that the killer shared with Grans. Haarmann later told the police that his lover had walked in unexpectedly while Franke's body was still warm. Confronted by the gruesome scene, Grans asked Haarmann a matter-of-fact question.

'When shall I come back again?'

Franke's murder marked the beginning of a spree. From that time on, Haarmann killed an average of one victim every three weeks. When he spotted likely young men at the railway station, he offered them employment and lodging. It was how he had met Grans. On several occasions he gained his victims' trust by passing himself off as a police detective. He then led them back to his apartment. Once there, the unfortunate young men would be killed and dismembered. Haarmann, who had received some training as a butcher, would sell what he could of his victims' bodies on the black market as meat. The remainder would be tossed into the River Leine.

Haarmann was both bold and cautious in his approach to murder. A good many people witnessed him openly leading boys and young men to his apartment; he even went so far as to visit the family of one of his victims in the hope of obtaining a reward. On the other hand, Haarmann was careful in that he preyed amost exclusively on runaways and others whose disappearance would never be noticed.

He would have gone on killing for a lot longer if he had not disposed of his victims' bodies so recklessly. On 17 May 1924, roughly 14 months into his killing spree, children playing near the banks of the Leine came upon a human skull. Twelve days later, the river washed up a second skull. During the following month, two more skulls were found in the sediment, along with more than 500 other body parts. Haarmann must have known of these discoveries, just as he must have been aware of the fear that was spreading through the city, yet he continued to kill without any change in his routine.

Ultimately, Haarmann's downfall was brought about by a boy he had decided not to kill. Karl Fromm was a 15-year-old male prostitute who had been picked up at Hanover station. He had once stayed for several days at Haarmann's apartment, during which time the pair had engaged in sexual activities. On 23 June, Fromm was plying his trade at the station when he got into an argument with Haarmann. The older man became so incensed that he told the railway police that Fromm was travelling on false papers. In turn, the boy accused Haarmann of molestation, a charge that led to his arrest.

Although fortune had shone on Haarmann back in 1918, this time it was the police that got a lucky break. As a sex offender, Haarmann was suspected of depositing the body parts in the River Leine, so his arrest on child molestation charges gave them the opportunity to investigate his apartment. When the investigators entered the premises they found a room filled with hundreds of articles of clothing that obviously belonged to boys and young men. Their problem was that they had no proof that Haarmann had murdered any of them – indeed, there was no evidence to indicate that any of them were dead at all. For his part, Haarmann would only admit to having had sexual relations with some of the boys and young men.

The case against the murderer might have stalled had it not been for a remarkable coincidence. One of the skulls from the River Leine had been identified as that of Robert Witzel, an 18-year-old who had gone missing on 26 April. His parents were summoned to the Hanover police station, where they were told the bad news. At that point, a man walked in wearing their dead son's jacket. When the man was approached by the grieving parents, he revealed that the article of clothing had been purchased from Haarmann.

Although the evidence was not conclusive, the Hanover police were certain that Haarmann was their killer. After seven days of interrogation, the used clothes salesman not only confessed, but he also agreed to lead his accusers to the locations of hundreds of other body parts. Throughout all of this, Grans had remained in Hanover. After being arrested on 8 July, he was charged on two counts of instigating murder. Grans' problems were serious enough, but they paled in comparison with Haarmann's, who had been charged with 27 counts of murder.

The court transcripts provide a revealing insight into Grans' and Haarmann's personalities. Where Grans comes off as cold and serious, Haarmann is by turn flippant, childish, boorish and excitable. The older man treated the courtroom as a stage. He enjoyed his starring role and went so far as to challenge the judge for the position of director. Haarmann once ordered the jury to come to a quick decision.

'Keep it short. I want to spend Christmas in heaven with my mother.'

He had no hesitation in describing the horrors that had taken place in the Neuestrasse apartment, including the very moment of death.

'I would throw myself on top of those boys and bite through the Adam's apple, throttling them at the same time.'

As each body cooled, Haarmann set to work harvesting the flesh that helped to support his modest lifestyle.

'I'd make two cuts in the abdomen and put the intestines in a bucket, then soak up the blood and crush the bones until the shoulders broke. Now I could get the heart, lungs and kidneys and put them in my bucket. I'd take the flesh off the bones and put it in my waxcloth bag. It would take me five or six trips to take everything and throw it down the toilet or into the river. I always hated doing this, but I couldn't help it – my passion was so much stronger than the horror of the cutting and chopping.'

Haarmann confessed to having killed 40 boys and young men in total. While on the witness stand, he attempted to take one more life – that of Hans Grans. He lied about his lover's participation in the murders, which resulted in Grans being found guilty of the 11 November 1923 murder of a 17-year-old apprentice named Adolf Hannappel.

We know that Grans was set up because of an odd letter that Haarmann wrote. He then threw it out the window of the car that was transporting him to the police station. Discovered by a courier, the four-page document takes the form of a confession. 'Hans Grans had been sentenced unjustly and that's the fault of the police and also because I wanted revenge.'

In another letter, Haarmann verifies his previous statement. 'You won't kill me; I'll be back – yes, I shall be amongst you for all eternity. And now you yourselves have also killed. You should know it: Hans Grans was innocent! Well? How's your conscience now?'

More than half a century passed before this particular document was discovered. It was unlikely that anyone connected with Grans' conviction was still alive – but if they were, they wouldn't have felt any guilt. When the first letter came to light, Grans' sentence was commuted to 12 years' imprisonment. After his release, Hans Grans returned to Hanover and dropped out of sight. He is believed to have lived until at least 1975.

On 15 April 1925, Fritz Haarmann was executed, as scheduled. The final words of this man who ended the lives of so many were: 'I repent, but I do not fear death.'

GARY HEIDNIK
The Basement and the Pit

Ellen Heidnik drank during her pregnancies. She drank a lot. Even at a time when the sight of a pregnant woman holding a wine glass was not unusual, Ellen stood out from the crowd. By the time her first child, Gary, was born – on 22 November 1943 in Eastlake, Ohio – Ellen's alcoholism had already begun to affect her marriage. Two years and one son later, her husband filed for divorce.

The effects of the split overshadowed Gary's early years, as well as his brother Terry's. Initially, the two boys stayed with their unstable, unreliable mother, but when she remarried they were sent to live with their father, Michael Heidnik, and his new wife.

As a boy, Gary Heidnik was traumatized by his mother and brutalized by his father

Misshapen head

They were very unhappy times for Gary. He disliked his stepmother and he was brutalized by his disciplinarian of a father. He was often punished for wetting his bed and suffered further when his father hung the stained sheets out of the second-floor bedroom window for all the neighbours to see.

Horrendous as this experience was for Gary, it was nothing compared to the terror he felt when Michael dangled him by his ankles in place of the sheets.

School was no better. Gary was not only taunted for the bed-wetting – he was also mocked because of his unusual appearance. As a young child he had fallen out of a tree, which had left him with a slightly misshapen head. Michael made his son's schooldays all the worse by painting bull's-eyes on the seat of his trousers, thereby creating a target for the bullies. In spite of all of these drawbacks, Gary excelled in the classroom. He was invariably at the top of his class and his IQ was once measured at 130.

His intelligence, combined with his status as an outcast, might have contributed to his unusual ambitions. While so many of his male classmates dreamed of becoming baseball players and stars of football, 12-year-old Gary's twin aspirations were the achievement of great wealth and a career in the military. He made an early start by entering Virginia's Staunton Military Academy at the age of 14. Once again Gary proved to be an excellent student. However, unlike Barry Goldwater and John Dean, two of the school's illustrious alumni, Gary never graduated from the prestigious school. After two years of study he left the academy, returning to his father's house. He attempted to resume his studies at a couple of different high schools but he felt that he was learning nothing, so at the age of 18 he dropped out of school and joined the army.

Though he made few friends amongst his comrades, Gary shone in the military. After completing basic training, he was sent to San Antonio in Texas, where he was to become a medical orderly. Now that his military career seemed well and truly on its way, Gary began pursuing his other long-held dream – to become wealthy. He supplemented his pay by making loans with interest to his fellow soldiers. Though his modest business would have been frowned upon by his superiors, Gary was otherwise an exemplary and intelligent military man. In 1962, while at a field hospital in West Germany, he achieved a near-perfect score in his high school equivalency examination.

A few months later it was all over.

In August, Gary began to complain of nausea, dizziness and blurred vision. The doctors who attended him identified two causes – stomach flu and 'schizoid personality disorder'. Before the year was up, he had been shipped back home. He was granted an honourable discharge and a disability pension. With one of his two dreams dashed into smithereens, Gary enrolled at the University of Pennsylvania. His chosen courses – chemistry, history, anthropology and biology – were so diverse in nature that it appeared that he was looking for direction. If so, Gary was unsuccessful. Using his army medical training, he worked for a time at two Philadelphia hospitals, but he proved to be a poor worker.

Now without work and living on his pension his eccentricities grew, while his personal hygiene declined. Gary found a leather jacket, which he would wear regardless of the weather or the social situation. If he did not want to be disturbed, he would roll up one trouser leg as a signal to others. Then there were the suicide attempts – not just Gary's, but those of his brother and his mother, too. These were so frequent that they could be numbered in the dozens, but only Ellen was successful. In 1970, the four-times married alcoholic took her own life by drinking mercury.

Both Heidnik boys spent years moving in and out of mental

institutions. Yet despite his many periods of confinement, Gary managed to begin amassing the wealth he had sought since he was a child. In 1971 he founded his own church, the United Church of the Ministers of God, and he ordained himself as its bishop. Although Gary had just four followers, they included two people who were close to him – his mentally retarded girlfriend and his brother.

On a roll

As a self-anointed minister, Gary began investing in earnest. He bought property and played the stock market, making a great deal of money when Hugh Hefner's Playboy empire went public in 1971. But all of the time he was spinning increasingly out of control. Gary became one of those individuals who is often described as 'known to the police'. There were any number of reasons for his notoriety. In 1976, for example, he used an unlicensed gun to shoot one of his tenants in the face. Incredibly, it was not until 1978 that he first went to jail. But the three- to seven-year sentence had nothing to do with the earlier shooting. Instead, Gary had been found guilty of kidnapping, unlawful restraint, false imprisonment, rape, involuntary deviate sexual intercourse and interfering with the custody of a committed person.

All of this had come about because Gary had signed his girlfriend's sister out of a mental institution and had kept her confined to his basement. Not only had he raped the young woman but he had infected her with gonorrhoea. In the middle of what turned out to be four years of incarceration, he handed a prison guard a note explaining that he could no longer speak because Satan had shoved a cookie down his throat. Gary remained silent for over 27 months.

When he was finally released in April 1983, he returned to Philadelphia and resumed his role as a bishop with the United Church of the Ministers of God. Even though Gary's congregation had not grown much, from time to time it included mentally retarded women, whom he would impregnate.

It is hardly surprising that Betty Disto, Gary's first bride, was not immediately aware of his odd behaviour and poor hygiene because the couple had become engaged before they had even laid eyes on one another. The couple had met through a matrimonial service. They had been corresponding for two years when, in September of 1985, Betty flew from her address in the Philippines to the United States. Their October marriage lasted for just three months. Betty could not stand to see her groom in bed with other women, but she had no choice because Gary made her watch. Beaten, raped and threatened, a pregnant Betty fled home with the help of the local Filipino community.

Betty made her escape in the first few days of 1986, but Gary's life really began to fall apart towards the end of that year. On the evening of 26 November 1986, Gary abducted his first victim, a prostitute named Josefina Rivera. It all happened gradually.

She had been standing outside in the cold rain when Gary picked her up in his Cadillac Coupe De Ville. On the way, he stopped at McDonald's and bought her a coffee. She did not object when he took her to his home, a run-down house at 3520 North Marshall Street.

There was something surreal about it all. Gary's house had seen better days, as had the rest of the neighbourhood. Decades earlier, the area had housed working-class German immigrants. The streets had been spotless then, but now they were pockmarked and covered in litter. Drug dealers worked its streets selling crack cocaine and marijuana to passing motorists and poverty was everywhere, yet Gary had a Rolls-Royce in his garage.

The door to his home was like something from a children's movie. When it opened, Josefina noticed that Gary had glued thousands of pennies to the walls of his kitchen. As he led her upstairs to the bedroom, she realized that the hallway had been wallpapered with $5 bills. In many ways, the house was a reflection of its owner. Gary's gold jewellery and Rolex watch contrasted sharply with his worn and stained clothing.

Like the rest of the house, the bedroom was sparsely furnished. There was nothing more than a waterbed, two chairs and a dresser. Gary gave Josefina the money they had agreed upon – $20 – and then he got undressed. The energetic and emotionless sex act was over in a matter of minutes. Josefina had felt a little uneasy about Gary, but what happened next took her by surprise. He grabbed her by the throat and choked her until she blacked out. Brief as it was, her loss of consciousness provided Gary with enough time to handcuff her.

Josefina was ordered to her feet and then she was marched downstairs to the basement. The unfinished room was cold, clammy and filthy, much like the old mattress that he made her sit on, and the floor was concrete, though some of the surface had been removed. After attaching metal clamps and chains to Josefina's ankles, Gary got down to digging the exposed earth. He talked as he worked, telling the shackled woman that he had fathered four children by four different women, but it had all gone wrong. He had no contact with any of his offspring and yet he really wanted and *deserved* a family.

'Society owes me a wife and a big family,' was how he put

it. 'I want to get ten women and keep them here and get them all pregnant. Then, when they have babies, I want to raise those children here too. We'll be like one big happy family.'

And with that bit of information, he raped her.

Screaming blue murder

Once she was alone, Josefina tried to escape. After freeing one of her ankles, she managed to prise open one of the basement windows and squeeze through it. Then she was out in the open. She crawled as far as the chain around her other ankle allowed her to and then she screamed at the top of her voice. But in Gary's neighbourhood screams like Josefina's were an everyday thing. The only person who paid any attention to the sound was Gary.

He ran downstairs, grabbed the chain and pulled her back into the basement. The filthy mattress was too good for her now. Dragging her across the cement floor, he threw her into the shallow pit. She was covered over with a sheet of plywood, upon which Gary placed heavy weights.

On her third day of captivity she was joined by a mentally retarded young woman named Sandra Lindsay. The girl seemed to have a very limited understanding of what was happening, so it was easy for Gary to get her to write a short note home. *'Dear Mom, do not worry. I will call.'*

It was the last time Sandra's mother would ever hear from her daughter.

Josefina and Sandra spent weeks together. Sometimes they were in the pit and sometimes they were chained to pipes in the basement. They endured repeated rapes, beatings and the ever-present cold.

On 22 December they were joined by 19-year-old Lisa Thomas, a third 'wife'. Gary lured the girl to 3520 North Marshall Street with offers of food and clothing and a trip to Atlantic City. In the end she only got the food and a spiked glass of wine. After she passed out, Gary raped her and then took her down to the basement.

On New Year's Day Gary abducted a fourth woman, but 23-year-old Deborah Dudley was totally unlike his other 'wives'. Ignoring the consequences, she fought back at nearly every opportunity. Her disobedience invariably led to the three other captives being beaten as well, which created disorder and tension within the group.

When Gary began to encourage the women to report on each other, Josefina saw an opportunity to gain Gary's trust. Though she continued to suffer at his hands, Gary came to believe that Josefina actually took pleasure in her circumstance.

Wife number five, 18-year-old Jacqueline Askins, arrived on 18 January. After raping and shackling the girl, Gary surprised his 'wives' with generous helpings of Chinese food and a bottle of champagne. After weeks of bread, water and stale hot dogs, it seemed like the most elaborate feast.

To what did they owe this unexpected treat? It was Josefina's birthday.

Wicked punishment

However, any hopes that Gary might be softening were soon dashed. If anything, his abuse escalated. When he caught Sandra Lindsay trying to remove the plywood covering from the pit, she was forced to hang by one of her wrists from a ceiling beam.

She responded by going on a hunger strike, but after a few

days she appeared incapable of eating. When Gary tried to force food down her throat, she vomited.

By 7 February, Sandra had completely lost consciousness. At this point, Gary finally removed the handcuff that had kept her dangling and she fell into a heap on the concrete floor.

Kicking her into the pit, he assured his other wives that Sandra was faking. It was probably a matter of minutes later that Sandra died.

The women watched as Gary carried Sandra's body upstairs and then they heard the sound of a power saw. Later that day, one of his dogs entered the basement. In its mouth was a bone covered in fresh meat.

Within days, the house and the basement took on a foul odour. Gary was finding it hard to dispose of Sandra's remains. Using his food processor he ground up what he could, feeding the meat to his dogs and his wives – but some body parts were very difficult to deal with.

Sandra's severed head sat in a pot of boiling water for days, while her rib cage was broiled in the oven. The smell spread to some of the adjoining properties, which led to complaints from the neighbours. Although the police investigated they believed Gary's story that he had cooked some bad meat. Meanwhile, the torture endured by the women became even more intense. Gary began poking their ears with a screwdriver, in the belief that deaf wives would be easier to control. He also stripped the insulation from extension cords in order to shock his captives.

Josefina was not only spared these punishments, she became an administrator. On 18 March she helped with an elaborate method of torture. First of all the pit was flooded and then the other wives, still in chains, were forced into the water. After

that the plywood covering was put in place and weighed down. Finally, the bare wire of the extension cord was pushed through a hole, thereby electrocuting the women.

The second of these shocks killed Deborah Dudley. Her death marked a significant change in Gary's relationship with Josefina.

In his eyes, her participation in the torture, combined with Deborah's death, meant she could be blackmailed. That made her trustworthy – or so he thought. For the first time in almost four months she was allowed to leave the basement. She shared Gary's bed, dined with him at restaurants and helped with his grocery shopping. Josefina even went so far as to accompany Gary to the country, where he disposed of Deborah's body.

On 24 March 1987, the day after she helped abduct a new woman, Agnes Adams, Josefina convinced Gary to let her visit her children. She promised him that she would return with yet another 'wife'. Gary dropped her off and waited in the car for her return. But Josefina did not visit her children – she had none. Instead, she sprinted to her boyfriend's apartment, where she poured out her bizarre and almost unbelievable story.

After the police arrived and noted the scarring that had been left by months of wearing heavy chains, they arrested Gary. His surviving 'wives' were rescued when the police converged on 3520 North Marshall Street on the following morning.

Gary's trial began on 20 June 1988. From the start, his defence lawyers attempted to prove that the one-time medical assistant was insane. They called a psychiatrist and a psychologist to the stand, but their efforts were in vain. Ten days later he was found guilty of two counts of first-degree murder, four counts of aggravated assault, five counts of rape, six counts of kidnapping and one count of involuntary deviate sexual intercourse. He was subsequently sentenced to death.

On the evening of 6 July 1999, 11 years after he had been sentenced, Gary Heidnik was executed by lethal injection. It is hardly surprising that his body was not claimed by the other members of his family.

Michael Heidnik, his father, had not seen him since the early 1960s. When he heard about the death sentence he made a brief statement to the press.

'I'm not interested. I don't care. It don't bother me a bit.'

H. H. HOLMES
The Doctor's Monster Castle

The most prolific American serial killer of the 19th century – perhaps the most prolific of all time – H. H. Holmes maintained that he was not accountable for his crimes. 'I was born with the devil in me,' he told the detectives who interrogated him. 'I could not help the fact that I was a murderer, no more than the poet can help the inspiration to sing. I was born with the evil one standing as my sponsor beside the bed where I was ushered into the world and he has been with me since.'

Holmes' association with the devil began on 16 May 1861 in the small town of Gilmanton, New Hampshire. His true name was Herman Webster Mudgett.

The son of Levi and Theodate Mudgett, he was a descendant of the earliest settlers in the area. Over the generations, the

Holmes disfigured cadavers to make it appear that they had died in horrific accidents

Mudgetts had done well for themselves. However, by the time Herman entered the world it was a family in decline. His alcoholic father did little to reverse the trend. Herman suffered under his father's strict discipline, which often manifested itself in violence. School brought little in the way of sanctuary as Herman was a frequent victim of bullying.

In one particular incident, which took place when he was quite young, his schoolmates forced him to touch a human skeleton at the office of the town's doctor. The experience brought about an abrupt change in the boy's character. Once the victim of bullying, Herman now became a bully himself. Moreover, he found that the experience with the skeleton had robbed him of any fear of death or the macabre. Herman soon began capturing and killing small animals in order to study their bodies. By his late teenage years, the future serial murderer had decided upon medicine as his vocation.

Because he lacked the money to attend medical school, he became a teacher at the age of 16. It was during his second posting, in the nearby town of Alton, that he met Clara Lovering, a member of a well-to-do farming family. After the two had eloped, Herman's new wife paid for his medical studies at the University of Vermont.

But the school was not to his liking. Herman imagined a great future for himself – the modest school in the small city of Burlington could not provide the foundation he required.

In the summer of 1882, Herman took his wife west so he could enrol at one of the country's leading medical schools, the University of Michigan at Ann Arbor. There was nothing magnificent about his performance as a student, but then all he really needed was the certificate he would receive upon graduation. However, Herman did one thing of note – something which his professors were unaware of – he stole cadavers that had been used in anatomy classes. He then disfigured the corpses to make it appear that they had died in horrific accidents. All that remained was to distribute them around the city. When they were discovered, he collected on the insurance policies that he had taken out.

Just a few months after his graduation in 1884, Herman carried off his greatest swindle with the help of a student who was still studying at the university. The scheming pair split a total of $12,500, after which Herman abandoned Clara and their infant son and left Ann Arbor. He then disappeared, surfacing only to cheat individuals and companies out of even more money. In St Paul, Minnesota, he was supposed to act as the receiver of a bankrupt store, but he sold off the goods and then vanished with the proceeds. For a time he taught in a school in Clinton County, New York, but after running up a large bill for board and lodging and impregnating his married landlady, he ran off.

Convincing bedside manner

In 1885, he reappeared in Chicago as 'Dr Henry Howard Holmes'. As a fairly handsome man who was something of a dandy, he cut quite a figure in his adopted city. He set himself up as an inventor and then he took a job as a prescription clerk in a very healthy pharmacy owned by a terminally ill man, Dr E. S. Holton. The supportive and helpful Holmes endeared himself to the dying doctor's wife. When Holton died he offered to take the pharmacy off her hands. A legal document was drawn up in which Holmes promised to pay the grieving Mrs Holton $100 a month until the entire business had been bought.

How many payments did Holmes make? Perhaps none. Shortly

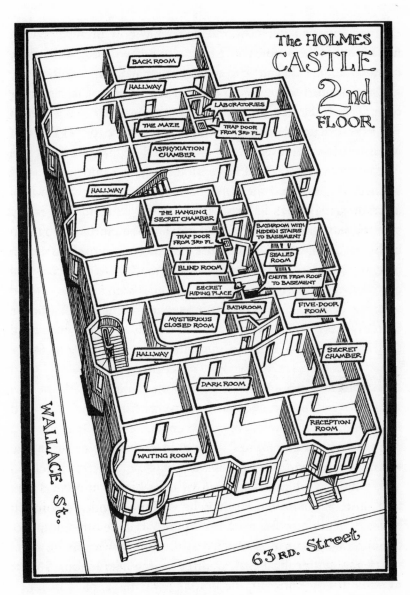

Overview of Holmes' maze of death

after signing the agreement, the doctor's widow disappeared. At first Holmes told people that Mrs Holton was visiting California, but then he said that she had fallen in love with the Golden State and had decided to stay. With Holmes at the helm, what had once been Dr E. S. Holton's pharmacy became healthier still. Chicago was experiencing a period of rapid growth and the former Herman Mudgett took full advantage of the boom times. Within two years of his arrival in the city, Holmes had become a wealthy man.

In 1887, he joined the ranks of the *nouveaux riches* with his marriage to Myrta Z. Belknap, the beautiful daughter of wealthy businessman John Belknap. It did not matter a bit that the groom had been married before because Holmes never told his bride. Nor did it matter that he was still married to Clara, because no one ever found out.

John Belknap provided Holmes with access to Chicago's business class, which he exploited to the full. Holmes even took advantage of John Belknap himself, by forging the old man's name on a number of deeds. The crime was exposed – and quickly hushed up – but Holmes' relationship with Myrta was already over. Though she had just given birth to their first and only child, Lucy, the marriage had run its course. The union had not been helped by Holmes' attempt to poison his father-in-law when the truth about his fraud was exposed.

What exactly Holmes wanted with all of the property he tried to acquire is unknown. Perhaps he was looking for a place to build. In 1889, he purchased an empty plot of land on the corner of South Wallace and West 63rd Street, directly across from his pharmacy, where he began a three-year construction project. Even as it was going up, the building was the subject of much talk in the neighbourhood. One block long and three storeys in height, the building's dominating presence earned it a nickname – 'the Castle'.

There was, however, another reason why the building was so often a topic of conversation. Dr Holmes was forever hiring and firing those who worked on its construction. There were two reasons for this behaviour. First of all, he saved money by dismissing someone every time he found some trivial flaw. The doctor would not pay for shoddy workmanship. Years later, investigators discovered that he had not paid one cent for the materials that had been used in the mammoth structure. Secondly, in having workers pass through what was in essence a revolving door, Holmes was able to keep secret the Castle's odd and eccentric design.

The ground floor of the building was conventional enough. A number of businesses were located there, including Holmes' relocated pharmacy, a sign painter and a vendor of used magazines. However, the upper two storeys were designed to resemble a maze. Features like trap doors, hidden staircases, secret passages and false floors abounded, and there were more than 100 rooms, most lacking windows.

Many of the doors could only be opened from the outside and other doors led to nothing but a brick wall.

Holmes completed the Castle just as Chicago was readying itself for the 1893 World's Columbian Exposition. His timing was excellent. Soon the city was swarming with tourists looking for a place to stay and Holmes was more than willing to oblige. As well as advertising his accommodation in the local newspapers he also offered employment to young ladies. The other advertisements he placed had nothing to do with business. He represented himself as a wealthy businessman in search of a suitable bride. Before long, the Castle was being visited by tourists, unemployed women and prospective mates. The building was once more a hive of activity, just as it had been when hundreds of workmen were coming and going. But this time around no one left.

Many visitors were asphyxiated in soundproof chambers that were fitted with gas pipes. Others met a similar fate after being locked in a bank vault that was located just outside Holmes' second-storey office. Once his victims were dead, he sent them sliding down any number of chutes located throughout the building. The bodies would end up in the Castle's basement, where Holmes would strip them of their flesh.

Many of the victims would end up as skeletons, much like the one he had been forced to touch as a child. He used his standing as a doctor to sell them to medical schools. Some bodies were cremated in one of the two gigantic furnaces that served to heat the Castle, while others were simply dropped into lime pits or vats of acid.

Holmes preyed almost exclusively on women, including Julia Connor, the wife of a jeweller to whom the doctor had rented a shop. Julia worked for both Holmes and her husband and she was also sleeping with both men. The situation suited Holmes, and it seemed just fine with Julia. But then he met a wealthy Texan named Minnie Williams. When the two became engaged, Julia told Holmes that she was pregnant with his child.

Holmes reacted to the news by killing Julia and her daughter Pearl. Julia's distraught husband trudged the streets of the city day and night, searching for his missing family.

Had Julia made a fatal mistake in standing up to Holmes? It does not seem so, if the doctor's statement to the investigators is anything to go by.

'I would have gotten rid of her anyway. I was tired of her.'

The commotion caused by Minnie's arrival at the Castle only seemed to intensify as time progressed.

When her sister came to visit she was seduced by Holmes, who encouraged her to sign over some property she owned in Texas. He then sent her tumbling down one of the chutes. When he married for a third time on 9 January 1894, the bride was not Minnie. How could it be? He had murdered her, too.

Holmes' third wife was Georgianna Yoke, yet another woman who had a good amount of money in the bank. Georgianna was under the impression that her husband was a very wealthy man. After all, he had a profitable pharmacy and he owned property in Texas and Illinois as well as the Castle. This was all true, though Holmes' fortunes had taken a turn for the worse. He had been living well beyond his means and he was dragged down with the American economy as it entered a recession. When his creditors came calling, there was little he could do. Though the doctor found it so very easy to kill a woman, he had little control over a bank.

After running through his new wife's money, he turned to swindling as a means of escaping debt. His first attempt was a fairly complicated scheme that involved horses, but it resulted in a brief period of imprisonment in St Louis. When he was released on bail, Holmes decided to return to the area he knew best, which was insurance fraud. His new scheme involved Benjamin Pitezel, a man whom he had employed as a carpenter while the Castle was being built.

Pitezel was a weak, simple-minded alcoholic who perhaps knew something of the horrors that had taken place in the Castle. What he made of them is a matter for conjecture.

Nevertheless, all of the evidence points to the fact that Pitezel had sufficient faculties to understand the swindle that Holmes had cooked up. The two men were to travel to Philadelphia, where the carpenter would establish himself as B. F. Perry, an inventor. Meanwhile, Holmes would take out a $10,000 insurance policy on his friend Perry. A few weeks later, there would be an explosion of such magnitude that a disfigured corpse would be all that remained of him.

According to the plan, Holmes would provide the necessary mutilated body. In the end, however, Holmes simply killed Pitezel.

Child killer

Following Pitezel's death, Holmes set off on a journey that can only be explained by the fact that the insurance company was on to him. After assuring Mrs Pitezel her husband was alive and well, the doctor talked her into letting three of her five children travel with him. Holmes moved from city to city and even crossed the border into Canada.

When the authorities finally caught up with him on 17 November 1894, he was in Boston.

He was charged with insurance fraud, which was a serious, but not insurmountable, charge. But then another question was asked. Where were the Pitezel children?

The answer came a few months later, when a diligent insurance agent located their small, unmarked graves in Indianapolis and Toronto.

The shocking news ruled out the possibility that Holmes might ever again be a free man.

On 20 July 1895 the Chicago police visited the Castle and

got their first glimpse of the secret horrors that had taken place within its walls.

It took only one day for the newspapers to change the building's nickname to the 'Murder Castle'. The investigators learned all they could about the labyrinth of rooms, secret passageways, chutes and stairwells, but most of the Castle's secrets would remain a mystery. On the evening of 19 August, 20 days into the investigation, the Murder Castle was destroyed in a sudden and intense blaze. No one knew what had caused it.

Before the fire destroyed all of the evidence, the police had tried to determine just how many people had been killed in the building.

In a century that knew nothing of DNA, it proved a frustrating activity. Body parts were scattered around the Murder Castle's basement and some were still floating in pools of acid.

Yet the investigators did notice some commonalities. For example, while some victims had been men and children, the great majority of them had been young, blond women.

Though Holmes admitted to only 27 murders, the true total is almost certainly much higher – some have gone so far as to peg it at 200. His confession was made through the Hearst newspaper chain, which had paid $7,500 for the exclusive rights. The printed statement also allowed the doctor to speak to a public that was calling for his life.

'Like the man-eating tigers of the tropical jungle, whose appetites for blood have once been aroused, I roamed about this world seeking whom I could destroy.'

On the morning of 7 May 1896, he would roam the world no more. He took his place on the trapdoor of the gallows without any apparent fear. Amiable to the end, he expressed only the wish that his death might be swift.

It was not to be.

Fifteen minutes after the trapdoor had been opened, H. H. Holmes was still alive, his body twitching. The man who had been born with the devil in him dangled on the end of the rope for 20 minutes before he died.

CAMERON AND JANICE HOOKER
The Box Under the Bed

Cameron Hooker seemed like a pretty regular guy. He was slightly gawky-looking and not particularly intelligent, but he was no dummy either. The most you could say about Cameron was that he was good with his hands. It was a skill that would enable him to pursue his fantasies and bring about a seven-year nightmare for one very unfortunate young woman.

Cameron was born in 1953 in the small Californian city of Alturas, though he spent much of his youth in the marginally larger community of Red Bluff. An unremarkable student, he began working at a local lumber mill while attending high school. He spent much of the money he earned on the sort of pornography that was produced for those with a leaning

Cameron Hooker kept his sex slaves in wooden boxes with the consent of his wife

towards sadism and masochism. Cameron kept his fantasies secret until the age of 19, when he met Janice. Four years his junior, she was a plain, shy, insecure high school girl with little experience of the opposite sex. Cameron believed that he had found someone who could be moulded to fulfil his desires. After a period of polite dating, he introduced Janice to a series of violent sexual acts, which involved bondage, flogging and near-asphyxiation.

In 1975, two years into the relationship, Cameron married Janice. However, even at the wedding, he had begun to tire of his teenage bride. Her submissive nature did not quite fit his fantasies. What Cameron wanted was a sex slave. And Janice? What did she want? Janice wanted a baby.

The young couple struck a bargain. Janice could have her child if Cameron could have a sex slave. Throughout his wife's pregnancy, the lumber mill worker built a number of wooden boxes, each of them designed to confine a victim and muffle their cries for help. Cameron went about his preparations with great care, all the while making sure that no one could see what was going on at the rented Red Bluff house. Such was his dedication that the arrival of the couple's child – Janice's child, really – did little to alter his plans. Cameron would not be rushed – everything had to be just right.

It was not until several months after the birth that Cameron went out and got his slave. Janice went along for the ride. Indeed, it might be said that she was used as a lure. Who would suspect a woman with a baby in her arms?

The woman that Cameron would call his slave was Colleen Stan, an attractive 20-year-old from Eugene, Oregon. On the morning of Thursday 19 May 1977 she left her home to visit a

Janice Hooker leaves court in Red Bluff, CA after giving testimony at a hearing

friend in Westwood, California, some 500 miles (800 km) to the south.

It did not worry Colleen that she had no car and little money, because she considered herself an experienced hitchhiker. By the middle of the afternoon the young woman had travelled nearly 350 miles (560 km) to Red Bluff, just an hour and a half west of her final destination. Colleen's arrival in this small Californian community marked the beginning of the final and most challenging leg of her trip. Up until this point, she had been travelling along the busy Interstate 5 (I-5), where rides were plentiful, but now she had to use the less-travelled State Route 36, which would take her into Westwood.

With the end of the journey in sight, the seasoned Colleen continued to show great caution, turning down the first two offers of rides. The third car to stop was Cameron's blue Dodge Colt. When she realized that the smiling man at the wheel was accompanied by a mother and child, all of her fears melted away. But Colleen gradually began to feel uneasy. She noticed that Cameron constantly stared at her through the rear-view mirror.

Under normal circumstances this type of warning sign would have prompted her to look for a way out. In fact, when the car stopped at a service station Colleen sought refuge in the toilets and considered escaping.

'A voice told me to run and jump out a window and never look back,' she later recalled.

But then there was the wife and the baby – surely the leering young man would not do anything with them around.

So Colleen returned to the car, unaware that she would not be free again for a long time. Just moments after pulling away from the service station, the Hookers talked about making a quick visit to some nearby ice caves. Cameron turned the Dodge on to a dirt road and after several minutes he brought it to a halt. The Hookers and their baby got out of the car, but Cameron returned. Jumping into the back seat, he pointed a knife at Colleen's throat. Terrified and fearing death, she allowed herself to be handcuffed, blindfolded and gagged. Cameron then locked a heavy, insulated plywood box around her head.

After Janice and the baby had returned to the car, Cameron turned it around and headed back to Red Bluff with his trophy – though he stopped for some fast food along the way. Once home, Cameron led Colleen into his basement, where he strung her up by the wrists before stripping off her clothing and whipping her.

Where was Janice in all of this? Presumably she was upstairs with the baby – though she came down to the basement to have sex with her husband as Colleen hung suspended in front of them. After the couple had finished, Cameron released Colleen's wrists and forced her into a coffin-like box. Then he once again locked the small plywood box around her head before leaving.

The initial horror that Colleen had experienced marked the beginning of a routine that consisted of whippings, beatings, choking, burning and electrocution.

When she was not being subjected to these tortures, Colleen was chained up in the larger of the two boxes. Eventually, Cameron constructed a small cell under the basement staircase, where he set his slave to work, shelling nuts and other menial tasks.

Weird contract

After seven months had passed, Colleen was presented with a contract stating that she agreed to become Cameron's slave.

Although it was just a simple piece of paper, the document marked the point at which Colleen's nightmare intensified. After he had forced her to sign the paper, Cameron told her that she had been registered with a body called 'The Slave Company'. It was a powerful organization, he claimed, whose operatives had the house under constant surveillance. Any act of disobedience would mean certain death for Colleen's relatives, he said.

Because she had signed the contract, Colleen – known simply as 'K' – was given access to the rest of the Hooker house. This meant nothing in terms of freedom. Instead, she was now charged with performing the household chores. Cameron continued to torture Colleen and he often interrupted her busy day to whip her.

Events soon took another dramatic turn when Cameron took Colleen into the master bedroom. However, any hopes he might have had of a *ménage à trois* were dashed when Janice refused to join in. Nevertheless, Cameron raped Colleen after his wife had left the marriage bed.

Things changed again when the family moved to a mobile home on an acre of land they had bought just outside Red Bluff. Having lost his basement, Cameron kept Colleen captive in a new box that slid under his waterbed. As Colleen lay in her box, the conception and birth of the Hookers' second child took place noisily above her.

Though Colleen spent more time in the box under the bed than in the coffin-like container at the old house, she was now allowed outside. She had contact with the neighbours and she even went jogging. It was only her fear of the Slave Company and what it might do to her family that prevented her from escaping.

Witnessing these examples of servitude, Cameron's confidence grew and his fantasies changed. In 1980, during the fourth year of captivity, he sent both his wife and his slave to a local bar to pick up men. When Colleen was not looking after the Hooker children, she was sent out into the streets of Reno and other communities to beg for money. Cameron's boldest move came when he had his slave write letters to her three sisters – they were the first signs they'd had that Colleen was still alive. Emboldened, he allowed a phone call and, eventually, a visit to her divorced parents in southern California.

On 20 March 1981, a thin, tired-looking Colleen was dropped off at her father's home. She had been gone for almost four years. It was a pleasant, if tense, visit. Little was said because her family were wary of driving her away. On the following morning, not long after she had attended church with her mother, Colleen was picked up by Cameron – or 'Mike' as he called himself. It was the name he had used three years earlier on the slave contract.

Back to square one

Colleen's return to the mobile home in Red Bluff marked yet another change in her circumstances. In many ways, it was a return to the treatment she had known when she had first been taken captive. Cameron bothered with her much less and the torturing became less frequent.

Colleen's days were now spent almost entirely in the box under the waterbed. Deprived of exercise and daylight, her hair began to fall out and she started to lose weight.

She listened as Cameron began talking to Janice about acquiring another slave – perhaps more than one. Cameron spent a good portion of the summer and autumn of 1983 digging a hole near the mobile home, so that a dungeon could be built.

After he had installed flooring and walls, it became Colleen's home. However, the underground chamber soon flooded, so Colleen was returned to her box.

After that failed experiment, Cameron came to the conclusion that he needed to move to a bigger place before he abducted more slaves. In order to achieve his goal, he sent Colleen to work at the local King's Lodge Motel. The young woman remained dutiful, telling co-workers nothing of her situation. Yet it was at the motel that Colleen's chains of captivity began to loosen. On 9 August 1984, she was picked up from work by Janice. The car trip home was anything but routine. Janice told Colleen that there was no Slave Company, no one was watching the mobile home and the contract was bogus. In short, every threat Cameron had used to keep her in bondage was a lie.

The torturer weeps

That evening, the two women planned Colleen's escape. By the next morning Colleen was on a bus to southern California, having been wired money by her father. Before leaving Red Bluff, she telephoned Cameron from the station. He cried when she told him that she was leaving. There would be more telephone calls in due course.

Although Colleen had told no one about her seven-year ordeal, she could not leave the Hookers behind. It was not long before she began calling Janice on a regular basis. She made 29 telephone calls in total, in which she encouraged Janice to leave Cameron. Colleen had grown bolder since she had discovered the truth about the Slave Company and she stood up to Cameron whenever he answered the phone. In tears, he pleaded with her to come back. The tables had turned.

After one abortive attempt, Janice did leave her husband, after making a full confession to her church minister, Pastor Dabney, who then telephoned the police. On 18 November, the Hookers were arrested. There would, however, be only one trial because Janice had been granted full immunity from prosecution in exchange for agreeing to testify against her husband. It took over ten months for Cameron's case to come to trial. He testified in his own defence, arguing that all sex acts with Colleen had been consensual. On 28 October 1985, Cameron Hooker was found guilty of kidnapping, rape and eight other offences. He was sentenced to a total of 104 years in prison.

JOHN T. JAMELSKE
The Threadbare Millionaire's Home-made Dungeon

John T. Jamelske was once a wealthy man, but now he is poor. His assets were sold off and divided among his victims – the five girls and women he abducted and kept as sex slaves. Now an old man, Jamelske began serving a sentence of 18 years to life in 2003. If he lives to be released – which is most unlikely – the rapist and kidnapper will walk out of prison with little more than the clothes on his back.

Jamelske was born on 9 May 1935 in Fayetteville, a small village in upstate New York. He was an acne-ridden adolescent and a bit of a loner, but there was nothing unusual or remarkable about his youth. When he became an adult he portrayed himself

John T. Jamelske with his wife Dorothy at the age of 26 – when his father died, he inherited a fortune

as a popular teenager, one who had dated the winner of the Miss New York Pageant, but his stories had no basis in reality. Although he was an unremarkable student, Jamelske managed to earn a university degree. In 1959, not long after graduation, he married Dorothy, an elementary school teacher. Jamelske never seemed to be able to hold down a steady job, but this hardly mattered. When his father died he inherited a good deal of money, along with a valuable collection of antique clocks. Their sale brought in a small fortune, which set Jamelske well on his way to becoming a millionaire.

It was not that Jamelske was an astute investor. The money he sank into real estate in Nevada and California brought in a good enough return, but his wealth is better explained by the fact that he was a remarkably cheap man.

Frugal to the extreme, he would gather coupons clipped out of newspapers in his local public library. The father of three boys, Jamelske wore tattered clothes and scoured the roadsides for discarded bottles and cans.

Jamelske's home was a modest bungalow in the New York town of DeWitt, not far from where he had grown up. It was littered with old cars, household appliances, tools, construction materials and furniture. In short, it was the lair of a packrat. On more than one occasion, the assortment of junk provoked unwanted attention from the town authorities.

In 1988, Jamelske sold a good percentage of his land to a local developer. Then he watched as a number of large expensive homes went up next to his, yet even though he was flush with cash he did nothing to improve his own property. The junk remained, much to the irritation of his new neighbours.

Abducted

That same year, Jamelske abducted his first victim, a girl he had encountered while cruising around nearby Syracuse in his old Mercury. After a few minutes of conversation, he managed to lure the 14-year-old, known only as 'Kirsten', into his car. He then drove to his mother's house, where he bound his victim with a heavy chain before lowering her into an old well. That day, 17 September 1988, marked the beginning of three years of sexual abuse by a man who was nearly four decades her senior. Jamelske controlled the girl by threatening that he would murder her younger brother if she did not submit to his wishes.

Ten months into her ordeal, Kirsten was moved to an underground bunker on Jamelske's property. It had been specifically built to hold his young victim. Jamelske's youngest son, Brian, helped him with the project, which was no small feat. It involved mechanical diggers and other assorted rented machinery. Jamelske told Brian – and his exasperated neighbours – that he was building a bomb shelter. The bunker, a two-roomed crude concrete structure that had no electricity or plumbing, was seen as just another manifestation of Jamelske's eccentric nature. Access was gained by crawling along a low, cramped tunnel that led from the garage. At the end of the tunnel was a heavy steel door.

Alarm

Kirsten's family and friends were alarmed at her disappearance, but they would have been even more concerned if they had known the truth. As it was, they took some comfort from the fact that she had run off in the past. Their fears were further put to rest when they received letters and phone calls from her over a two-year period, along with an audio tape. In some of them she announced that she would soon be coming home. As 1990 drew to a close, she did just that – but not before suffering one more bizarre ordeal.

Blindfolded, the girl was taken out of the bunker and taken by car to Syracuse Hancock International Airport.

The car's driver, Brian Jamelske, knew nothing about Kirsten, so to allay his suspicions he was told that she had been placed with his father in order to combat a weight problem. And the blindfold? That was just part of a practical joke. Once at the airport, a mere 15 minutes from the Jamelske home, Kirsten's blindfold was removed and she boarded a plane for Nevada, accompanied by her abductor.

Jamelske and Kirsten spent a week together at Lake Tahoe, at the end of which he handed her a plane ticket back to Syracuse. Kirsten flew back on her own, straight into the arms of a relieved family. She kept the truth about her time in captivity a secret, never letting on that she had done anything but run away from home.

Jamelske also returned to Syracuse, where he resumed his routine of collecting coupons, bottles and old junk. Four years went by before he found a replacement for Kirsten. On the evening of 31 March 1995, he was again cruising through the streets of Syracuse when he came upon another 14-year-old girl. He sat chatting to her for a few minutes and then he managed to get her into his car. On the pretext of giving her a small job that involved delivering a package, they drove to his home in DeWitt. There he overpowered the girl, forcing her into his bunker.

Like Kirsten before her, the girl suffered sexual abuse daily – with Jamelske now using Viagra and other anti-impotence drugs. Just as he had done with his previous sex slave, Jamelske told the girl that he would kill a member of her family if she did not co-operate. He added weight to his threat by producing photographs of her family home.

Out of the bunker

As with Kirsten, Jamelske decided to release this new girl after roughly two years. Once again he blindfolded his sex slave and led her out of the bunker. But there would be no trip to Lake Tahoe this time. Instead, the kidnapper simply drove the girl to her mother's Syracuse home. This time the family was told of the nightmare, but fear prevented anyone from going to the authorities. For some time after her return, the girl noticed Jamelske driving slowly past her mother's house.

On 31 August 1997, Jamelske took his third sex slave. Everything appeared to follow his normal routine. The victim was seen while he was cruising the streets of Syracuse, she got into his car willingly, she was driven back to his DeWitt home and she was forced into the bunker.

Jamelske kidnapped a 53-year-old woman and forced her to live in his bunker

The difference is that Jamelske's victim was 53 years of age, so she was considerably older than her predecessors. The woman was sexually abused for nine months before being driven to a bus station, where she was given $50 before being released.

This time the victim reported her abduction and the repeated assaults. But her statement was made to a sceptical police department. It seemed that the whole story was thrown into question by the mere fact of the woman's survival. As one detective reportedly told her, 'Usually, if someone gets kidnapped, they don't come home alive.'

Jamelske's abductions and all of the goings-on in his bunker had taken place under the nose of his wife, yet it is almost certain that she knew nothing of her husband's nightmarish activities. Dorothy Jamelske was a very sick woman who was bedridden with colon cancer. Her death in 1999 left Jamelske alone in the house, which meant that he could afford to be far less cautious.

He found his fourth sex slave, a woman who has identified herself only as 'Jennifer', on 11 May 2001. This time, the abductor found his victim in DeWitt, where she was a waitress in an Outback Steakhouse. The 26-year-old had just completed her shift and was walking home. When Jamelske pulled up to offer her a ride she was being followed by a group of men, so he must have looked like an angel in disguise. But not for long. Before the evening was out, she would find herself in the clammy concrete bunker.

Naked woman

Jamelske told Jennifer all sorts of stories to keep her submissive. On one occasion he claimed that the local police were involved in some sort of sex slave ring. As the third month of Jennifer's confinement approached, Jamelske made the naked woman get dressed. He then placed a hood over her head and led her to his car. After a short drive she was freed in front of her mother's house. Like Jamelske's previous victim, Jennifer went to the police. And as before, the investigation went nowhere.

His next victim, a 16-year-old girl, was picked up in October 2002. She spent the first month in the bunker, during which time Jamelske threatened her with imaginary dogs and claimed that others wanted to rape her. His growing confidence then led him to take unnecessary risks. Unlike the others, she was allowed to use the house. As the months passed, Jamelske took to parading his victim in public. The pair went shopping and bowling and they even spent an evening at a karaoke bar.

On 8 April 2003, Jamelske pushed his luck too far. He decided to take the girl with him to the local bottle depot. Once there, she telephoned her sister to say she'd been kidnapped and was being raped. It took minutes for the police to arrive in the area. The kidnapper was arrested at a nearby car dealership.

When the authorities visited Jamelske's house they found the dungeon that had been described to them so many years earlier.

Less sinister, but equally strange, was a ten-foot wooden pillar that supported a replica of a human head. And right in the middle of the mess of old furniture, appliances, books, magazines and assorted newspapers, they found more than 13,000 empty beer bottles neatly arranged by brand, size and colour – order within chaos.

Jamelske denied that he had done anything wrong when he was interviewed by the police. He believed that the women he had kidnapped and raped had benefited from the experience. And yet he chose to plead guilty in making a deal with the prosecutors.

In return for leniency, his assets would be sold off and divided amongst his victims. The heartless sex attacker looked old and frail rather than dangerous.

Two days after his 14 July 2003 court appearance, John T. Jamelske made the following statement to a reporter:

'I've always said, you know, I'm unorthodox. And I've said to hundreds of people, I'm a little bit crazy.'

JOACHIM KROLL
The Cannibal's Kitchen and the Communal Toilet

Joachim Kroll seemed such a simple, uncomplicated man.
How could he have been otherwise? After all, he had not
been blessed with brains. The five years of schooling he
had received had left him barely able to read. In middle age,
Kroll seemed to have settled into a comfortable, if slightly
lonely existence, dividing his time between his small flat and
his lavatory-cleaning job. One might wonder whether he was a
competent employee, because it was a blocked toilet that would
expose Kroll as the monster he really was.

Born on 17 April 1933 in the German city of Hindenburg,
now a part of Poland, Joachim Georg Kroll was the youngest
of eight children. He was considered the runt of the litter. The
description might have been cruel, but it did reflect one sad truth.

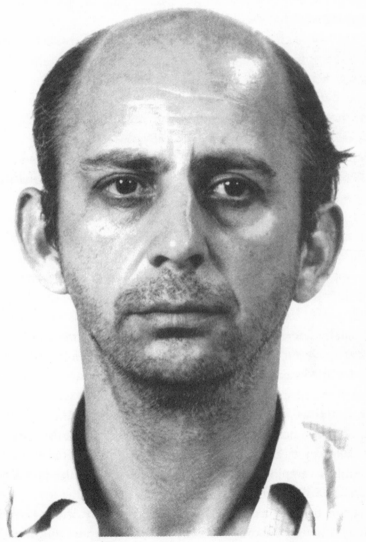

After school, Kroll was sent to work on a farm, where his mind was affected by animal slaughter

Young Joachim was not an intelligent child. In fact, his IQ had been measured at 76.

Despite his limitations, Kroll might have followed his father into the mines of Upper Silesia had it not been for the advent of the Second World War. His father fought on the eastern front before being taken prisoner by the Soviets and he never returned home. Two years after the fall of the Third Reich and the division of Germany, what was left of the Kroll family moved west, settling in North Rhine-Westphalia. Their new home was less than ideal. The adolescent Joachim found himself sharing a two-room flat with his mother and six sisters.

By this time, his schooling had ended. After struggling with his schoolwork for years he was barely literate, so it seemed futile to continue. It was just as well, because his mother needed his help in supporting the family. He was sent to work on a farm. Kroll would later say that he had been influenced by his involvement with the slaughter of animals. As the years passed, his sisters gradually left the cramped apartment to get married, which left more space for those who were left behind. When his mother died at the beginning of 1955, he was living alone with her.

Freed from his mother's influence and suddenly alone, his character changed. Eighteen days later, on 8 February, he murdered a young woman on the outskirts of the town of Lüdinghausen. It was not at all what the 21-year-old Kroll had intended. Over two decades later, he would tell the police that he had been on one of his many strolls through the local woods when he had come upon a 19-year-old runaway, Irmgard Strehl. He had invited her to join him, she had accepted and together they had left the trail and walked into the woods. The fact that Irmgard was a runaway might have had something to do with her willingness to spend time with Kroll. This is not to say that she was willing to exchange sexual favours for cash – Irmgard dodged when Kroll tried to kiss her. Enraged, he dragged her into a barn where he stabbed her in the neck, killing her almost instantly. Her fresh corpse was then raped and disembowelled.

Little else of note happened to Kroll during the rest of 1955. He continued to live alone, earning a modest living through farm work. In fact, he kept out of trouble until 1959. In that year he moved to the city of Duisburg, where he began working as a lavatory cleaner. It would be his occupation until he was put behind bars. The new home and the new job were soon followed by two new murders.

The first one took place on 16 June. Kroll approached 24-year-old Klara Frieda Tesmer while she was walking in a meadow on the banks of the Rhine. When she rejected his advances, he became angry. He hit her and choked her until she was dead and then he raped her dead body.

Ten days later he strangled 16-year-old Manuela Knodt in a densely-wooded park. Following his by now familiar pattern, he raped the dead girl's body. However, this time he removed parts of her thighs and buttocks as a trophy. Before leaving the scene, he masturbated over her disfigured corpse. Kroll would one day tell the police that he had harvested the flesh from Manuela's body because he could rarely afford to buy meat. He also admitted that he wanted to see what cooked human flesh tasted like.

It was not only Manuela and her grieving family who were the victims of Kroll's horrific crime. A mechanic named Heinrich Ott was found guilty of the girl's murder after he had been wrongly arrested. Distraught at being sentenced to eight years in prison, he ended up hanging himself in his cell.

Despite his low IQ, Kroll was cunning enough not to take risks. When the urge to kill took him over he would make a point of taking a bus or a train to an isolated rural area. This simple plan decreased his chances of being caught in the act and made it less likely that the police would link the murders to the same killer.

Erratic pattern

Kroll's erratic killing pattern also fooled the authorities, though he might not have planned it that way. Beginning with Irmgard Strehl in 1955, he killed a total of 13 victims over a period of just over 21 years.

In several of those years he murdered twice, while in 14 others Kroll committed no murders at all. There was also the matter of his victims' ages. Kroll did not care how old his victims were as long as they were female.

As a result, their ages ranged from 4 to 61, which is an unusually wide span for a serial killer.

Kroll claimed one male victim – 26-year-old Hermann Schmitz – but that was only because he got in the way. He met his end on 22 August 1965 at the side of a small lake outside Duisburg. Schmitz had driven to the secluded spot so that he could be alone with his girlfriend, Marion Veen, but Kroll had spotted his Volkswagen – and Marion. To get to the girl it was clear that he would have to kill her male companion. Kroll forced Hermann to exit the Volkswagen by sticking a knife into one of its tyres. Hermann was murdered as soon as he left the car, but the rest of Kroll's scheme did not go according to plan. Marion quickly jumped into the driver's seat and began honking the horn. Then she sped away. Kroll fled into the woods, leaving

Hermann's body untouched on the shore. He had no interest in eating male flesh.

The cannibal killer often claimed that the timing of his killings was determined by an uncontrollable desire. His urge to kill might grow for years, or just days, before it became unbearable. At that point, the only way to sate his desire was to kill a female. But Marion's escape could hardly have satisfied his urges, so why did the lavatory attendant not attempt to kill again for more than a year?

Wrong place, wrong time

Twenty-year-old Ursula Rohling was his next victim, though Kroll would not have known her name or her age. The young woman he killed on 13 September 1966 was a stranger, just like the others. She had simply been in the wrong place at the wrong time. Her body was discovered in the brush that bordered a park trail outside the town of Marl, roughly 49 km (30 miles) north-east of Kroll's Duisburg home. Ursula had spent the hours leading up to her death with her fiancé, Adolf Schickel. The young couple had been sharing an ice cream while they went over their wedding plans.

Once Ursula's body had been found, the weight of suspicion fell immediately on Adolf. After all, he was the only person to have been seen in her company that evening. Suffering from the loss of his future bride and the strain of weeks of interrogation and accusations, Adolf committed suicide by throwing himself into the Maine.

Adolf Schickel, Hermann Schmitz and Heinrich Ott were not the only men to die as a result of Kroll's murderous activities. On 4 June 1962, Kroll murdered 12-year-old Monika Tafel, but no one looked in his direction. Instead, a 34-year-old man named Walter Quicker was arrested for the crime. He was not charged, but he killed himself after being ostracized and targeted by his neighbours after his release.

Yet another man, Vinzenz Kuehn, was made to pay the price for Kroll's crimes. He was found guilty of the murder of Petra Giese, whom Kroll had killed on 23 April 1962. While Kuehn was wasting away in a prison cell, Kroll still walked free.

In spite of all his years of killing, Kroll had never been regarded as a suspect. In fact, the lavatory cleaner had never once crossed paths with the police. His cover was nearly blown in June 1967, when he encouraged 10-year-old Gabriele Püttman from the town of Grafenhausen to accompany him to a nearby meadow. Kroll had promised to show her a rabbit, but instead he produced a pornographic magazine. He grabbed her when she tried to run and had just begun choking her when a nearby coal mine changed shifts. The woods became flooded with men on their way home, so Kroll fled and the girl survived. Kroll had been taking a risk by attacking the 10-year-old. He had been living in Grafenhausen on a temporary basis and had not followed his previous method of targeting victims far from home.

By the end of the year Kroll was back working in Duisburg. He found an apartment at number 11 Friesenstrasse in the suburb of Laar. It was a modest flat that did not even have its own bathroom. That did not matter. With three rooms, the flat seemed luxurious when it was compared with the one in which he had lived with his mother and sisters. Kroll was more than content to share a lavatory with the other tenants.

A quiet period followed Kroll's return to Duisburg but everything changed on 12 July 1969, when he raped and strangled his oldest victim, 61-year-old Maria Hettgen, in the town of Hückeswagen. A year later, he raped and murdered 13-year-old Jutta Rahn in the town of Breitscheid. Her death would lead to yet another wrongful conviction.

After he had murdered Jutta, the urge to kill left Kroll for quite some time. There were no more victims for over six years.

Then, in the summer of 1976, Kroll left his home and travelled some 23 km (15 miles) north to the town of Voerde, where he raped and strangled a 10-year-old named Karin Toepfer.

Joachim Kroll was now a middle-aged man. After nine years of living in his modest Laar flat, he had become a popular figure with the neighbourhood children. He would give them sweets and tell them jokes. 'Uncle Joachim', as he came to be known, would even invite them into his apartment where he had a collection of dolls and small toys. He took delight in watching the children play, particularly the girls.

Parents were not troubled by the attention Kroll was giving the children, nor did anyone complain that they were playing in his flat, even though it was a clear violation of the building's rules. In their eyes, he was a harmless old bachelor. Who would deny the old man a break from his loneliness? Besides, the children loved their funny 'uncle'.

So when 4-year-old Marion Ketter vanished while playing in a local park on 3 July 1976, no one cast a suspicious eye at Kroll. It was not until the next day that the police reached number 11 Friesenstrasse. Their arrival was well-timed. As they opened the door they bumped into an agitated man, who was rushing out to get help.

Oscar Muller's state of panic was perfectly understandable. Just moments before, he had been on his way to use the communal lavatory when he had encountered Joachim Kroll. The toilet was blocked, his neighbour told him… with guts. Muller thought Kroll was joking, until he entered the room. To his horror, the lavatory was full to overflowing with a bloody liquid and what appeared to be floating flesh. The police sealed off the room and waited for a medical examiner and a plumber. It appeared that the toilet bowl contained the heart, lungs, kidneys and intestines of a young child. They were looking at the remains of Marion Ketter.

Kroll was unfazed by all the activity taking place down the hallway from his flat. When the police officers asked him about the blocked toilet, he told them that he had caught and killed a rabbit in order to make a stew. He had attempted to dispose of the animal's internal organs by flushing them down the toilet.

As they stood in Kroll's doorway, the police could smell a home-cooked meal. When they entered the flat they found that there was indeed a stew simmering on the stove. A detective then picked up a spoon so that he could check out the ingredients. Before he did so, Kroll quickly admitted that his recipe included pieces of the missing 4-year-old. A severed hand and small chunks of human flesh were found floating among the vegetables. Kroll's refrigerator and freezer yielded up more pieces of the girl.

At first, Kroll would only admit to the murder of Marion Ketter, but the longer he remained in custody the more he relaxed. After a few days, it seemed that Kroll had become quite taken with life behind bars. He began to talk openly about the murders he had committed over the past two decades. The lavatory attendant even offered to give the detectives a tour of the various locations at which he had killed and butchered his victims.

Cooked flesh

He told the police that once he had sampled the cooked flesh of Manuela Knodt, back in 1959, he had not been able to return to a strictly non-human diet. In fact, he had stalked the girls and women who had looked as though they would provide the tastiest morsels. True, he had left some of his victims with their corpses intact, but this was only because he did not think their meat would appeal to his taste buds.

It was good to get all of this out into the open, Kroll told the police. Now would they please fix him? Kroll naively believed that he would neither pay a penalty nor endure a punishment for the 13 murders he had committed. He simply thought that he would undergo a simple, painless surgical procedure and be released. The news that he would be going before a judge and jury came as a bit of a shock. Kroll was charged with eight of the murders to which he had confessed.

His trial began on 4 October 1979 and lasted until 8 April 1982, when he was sentenced to life imprisonment. In his case, life meant little more than nine years. He died of a heart attack on 1 July 1991 at the age of 58.

CHARLES NG AND LEONARD LAKE
The Operation Miranda Bunker

When it is compared to the horrific crimes that have been committed by Charles Ng, shoplifting seems such a trivial offence. Yet the simple theft of a bench vice was enough to seal Ng's fate and that of his partner in crime, Leonard Lake.

Ng was born in Hong Kong on Christmas Eve, 1960, to a wealthy, if unstable, family. His father, a highly-placed company executive, maintained discipline through constant beatings. The adolescent Ng was a poor student with no real friends, so he distinguished himself by attacking and beating younger children. At the age of 15 he was caught shoplifting for the first time. He

Leonard Lake loved animals, but when his pet mice died he dissolved their bodies in acid

was then sent to an English boarding school, but he was expelled after setting fire to a classroom.

At the age of 18 he moved to the United States, where he attended Notre Dame de Namur University, a small Catholic institution that is located in Belmont, California. He lasted just one semester.

Despite his dismal academic background, Ng was accepted into the United States Marine Corps in 1980. Less than a year later, he was caught stealing various kinds of weapons, including machine guns, from the Hawaiian base at which he was stationed. His attempt to escape added a charge of desertion to his record. After being dishonourably discharged, he was sentenced to 14 years in a military prison, but was released in late 1982.

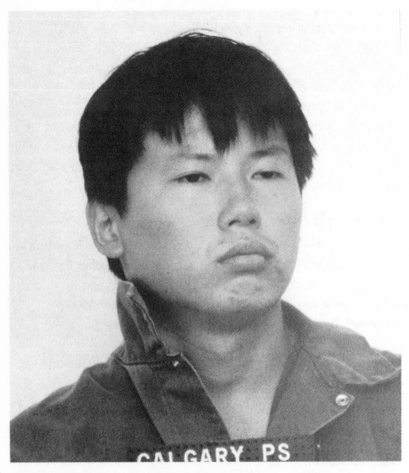

Charles Ng was thrown out of school for arson and then dishonourably discharged from the Marines

Ng's bad experience with the Marines was something he shared with Leonard Lake. Born on 29 October 1945 in San Francisco, Lake had not enjoyed anything like Ng's privileged childhood. His parents had separated when he was 6 years old, which resulted in the Lake children being sent to live with their grandparents. Unlike Ng he had been a fairly good student as a child. He had also pursued some odd hobbies. He kept mice and, when they died, watched with interest as he dissolved their bodies in acid. He also enjoyed taking nude photographs of his sisters, an activity that was encouraged by his grandmother. His favourite book was *The Collector* by John Fowles, a novel about a seemingly mild young man who imprisons an attractive art school student, Miranda Grey, while he tries to make her love him.

Personality disorder

Lake was 19 when he joined the Marines. He completed two tours of duty in Vietnam as a radar operator, but he was discharged in 1971 after having been diagnosed with schizoid personality disorder. Once more a civilian, he enrolled in San José State University, but he lasted only one semester. Lake's 1975 marriage was equally brief. It ended when his wife learned that he had been making amateur pornographic films. Even worse, he had been starring in them. He remarried in 1981, though his return to marital status was brief. His second wife did not want to act in his pornographic films, most of which featured bondage and sadomasochism. By the time he was arrested on a firearms violation in the following year, Lake had already gone through his second divorce.

It was Lake's second brush with the law. He had already served some time for car theft and he had no intention of returning to prison. Skipping bail, he hid out on an isolated property in Calaveras County, California, that belonged to his wife. It was not long before Lake met Charles Ng. They were both visiting San Francisco's red-light district at the time. The two men immediately recognized each other as kindred spirits. Among other things they shared a common interest in firearms and other weapons, as well as a belief in a coming nuclear holocaust.

Before long, Ng joined Lake in Calaveras County, where he assisted him in setting up 'Operation Miranda', a project that was named after the woman who had been held captive in *The Collector*. Leonard Lake explained the plan in a video he had made of himself in October 1983, shortly before his 38th birthday.

> *'What I want is an off the shelf sex partner. I want to be able to use a woman whenever and however I want. And when I'm tired or bored I simply want to put her away.'*

To this end, the pair built a bunker in the side of a hill. It was intended as the first of many that would house the pair's sex slaves. The women would be used to repopulate the planet after the expected nuclear war. Crudely constructed, it consisted of a main room that contained power saws and the other tools that were needed for disposing of bodies. There was also a smaller, sparsely-furnished room. Beneath it there was a cramped, windowless cell, which could be accessed through a trapdoor in the floor. On its walls were photographs of the young women that Lake and Ng had abducted, tortured, raped and killed.

The pair had also murdered a number of men and children – usually those who had been with the women when they were captured.

Most of the victims' bodies were burned in a home-made crematorium that had been built beside the bunker. Exactly how many people Ng and Lake killed is unknown, though the number is usually estimated at between 15 and 25. What can be said with more certainty is that Operation Miranda came to an end on 2 June 1985.

On that day, customers at a San Francisco hardware store noticed Ng stealing a bench vice. Police officers caught sight of the former Marine as he was putting the stolen item in the back of a Honda, but he managed to flee on foot. Lake had been sitting at the wheel, so he was easily apprehended. He was taken to the local police station where a quick search uncovered a revolver, complete with silencer.

As the detectives prepared to question their suspect, the driving licence he provided was run through the system. The name on the document, Robin Scott Stapley, was that of a man who had been missing for nearly four months. It was then discovered that the Honda was registered to Paul Cosner, a man who had disappeared in the previous November while delivering the vehicle to a prospective purchaser.

While he was waiting in the interrogation room, Lake asked for a pencil, a sheet of paper and some water. Minutes later, he was found slumped in his chair, barely alive.

He was rushed to hospital, where it was discovered that he had swallowed cyanide pills. He died four days later. The pencil and paper had been used to write one last letter to his second wife, the owner of the Calaveras County property:

Dear Lyn,
I love you. I figure your Freedom is better than all else.
Tell Fern I'm sorry. Mom, Patty and all. I'm sorry for all
the trouble.
Love
Leonard

After Lake's death, investigators from the local sheriff's office visited his isolated mountain home. There was some suspicion that he and Ng had been trading in stolen goods. They had, after all, been advertising used items for sale. One look at the house was enough to make them realize that petty theft was the least of their crimes. The living room ceiling was stained with blood and there were bullet holes here and there. In the master bedroom, the investigators found a collection of lingerie, much of it stained with blood. The mattress on the bed was also stained and electrical cords had been tied to the bedposts.

After searching the grounds, the investigators found ashes, teeth and human bones buried in a long trench. Because the act of cremation had made identification difficult, the authorities relied on other clues. For example, Lake had been trying to sell some furniture that belonged to his neighbours. He explained that the items had been left as payment for a debt when they had moved to Los Angeles. Yet, those same neighbours – Lonnie Bond, his girlfriend Brenda O'Connor and their baby – were nowhere to be found.

An impressive array of expensive video equipment was found in the house. It was traced back to Harvey and Deborah Dubs, a young couple who had disappeared from their San Francisco home in the previous year. Their 16-month-old son was also missing.

Among the victims that the police were able to positively identify was Donald Lake, Leonard's brother.

After two weeks, the police had discovered nine bodies and nearly 18 kilograms (40 pounds) of charred teeth and bones. Though it was painstaking work, which involved dozens of people sifting through tons of soil, some progress had at least

Jim Stenquist, Calaveras County information officer, reveals the bunker's secret entrance

been made. The same could not be said about the hunt for Charles Ng. Like his many victims, he seemed to have vanished. Could it be that Ng, too, had taken his own life?

Fugitive

In fact, Ng was very much alive. He had fled some 1,500 km (940 miles) to the north, where he had managed to cross the border into Canada. On 6 July 1985, after he had been on the run for more than a month, he was spotted shoplifting in a downtown Calgary department store. When he was approached by two male security guards, Ng pulled out a revolver and shot one of the men in the hand. Incredibly, the injured guard still managed to overpower the former Marine and keep him restrained until the police arrived.

It did not take the Canadian authorities long to identify Ng, but his extradition created a legal problem. Canada was a country that had abolished capital punishment, so the authorities were reluctant to send Ng back to California, where the death penalty was still in force. That is not to say that Ng was a free man. In December 1985 he was sentenced to four-and-a-half years in prison for shooting the department store security guard. As Ng sat in a Canadian prison, American lawyers fought to have him returned to the United States. One of the arguments was that Canada risked becoming a safe haven for criminals who faced the death penalty at home.

Then on 26 August 1991, the Supreme Court of Canada ruled that Ng could be extradited. Minutes after the ruling, the murderer was on a flight back to the United States. Ng's trial did not begin until October 1998, more than 13 years after his last murder. Eight months later, he was found guilty of the murder of three women, six men and two babies. He was sentenced to death. In 1999, pending appeal, he took up residence on San Quentin Prison's Death Row.

DENNIS NILSEN
The Army Butcher's Attic Home

By February 1983, the house at 23 Cranley Gardens in the north London suburb of Muswell Hill had seen better days. Once a charming family home, it had been divided into flats, some more finished than others. The attic flat, for example, lacked floorboards. However, while the house was not looking its best, it was not exactly in disrepair either. When problems began to develop with the lavatories, the owner quickly hired a plumber. And when the plumber was unable to solve the problem, a drain-cleaning company was brought in. It was Michael Cattran, a Dyno-Rod employee, who exposed Dennis Nilsen as one of the most active serial killers in British history.

Nilsen was born on 23 November 1945, in the seaside town of Fraserbugh, Scotland. His Scottish mother and Norwegian father divorced when he was 4 years old, after which he rarely saw his father. Most of his early years were spent being shunted backwards and forwards between his mother and his grandparents. At school, his studies were hindered by his developing homosexual feelings, which made him feel confused and guilty, so he left as soon as he could. In 1961 he enlisted in the army as a boy soldier and four years later he joined the Catering Corps, where he was trained as a butcher.

Nilsen's service took him to West Germany, South Yemen, Cyprus, the Gulf of Oman and Scotland. However, when he was posted to Northern Ireland in 1970, his attitude towards the army changed. After having served for a decade, he resigned from the forces and took a job as a security guard. A year's stint with the Metropolitan Police Force followed. Nilsen would later say that he had submitted his resignation because he did not like arresting homosexuals. In March 1974 Nilsen joined the Department of Employment. He proved himself to be a conscientious, reliable worker, who was willing to accept long hours without complaint. Outside work, however, his behaviour was becoming increasingly unstable. Nilsen's long-standing fascination with death, which he traced back to viewing his grandfather's corpse at the age of 6, had morphed into necrophilia. He spent hours making up his face to look like a corpse, after which he would stare at himself in the mirror.

In 1975, at about the time of his 30th birthday, Nilsen became friendly with a 20-year-old named David Gallichan. The two men set up home in an attractive flat at 195 Melrose Avenue in north London. Gallichan, who had always denied that their relationship was homosexual, would leave after two years. Heartbroken and lonely, Nilsen began picking up young men for casual sex. He would later admit that he had killed in order to satisfy his need to commit acts of necrophilia. Although Nilsen could not remember how many people he had killed, he was fairly certain that the first murder had been committed on 30 December 1978. Stephen Dean Holmes, an Irish teenager, had been picked up in a gay bar on the previous evening. He was strangled in the morning as he made to leave.

Nilsen had wanted the young man to stay – the thought of spending New Year's Eve alone was unbearable. In order to make certain that Holmes was dead, he immersed his head in a bucket of water. He then cleaned the body, dressed it in fresh underwear and lay in bed with it.

Almost a year went by before Nilsen killed again. Then in December 1979 he picked up Kenneth Ockendon, his second victim. Ockendon was a 23-year-old student who was due to fly home to Canada the next day. As before, Nilsen did not want the young man to go, so he strangled him with the cord of his headphones. Of all his victims, Ockendon seemed to have had a special place in Nilsen's heart, perhaps because they got along so well.

Nilsen followed his usual routine by having sex with Ockendon's corpse, but he also took photographs, drew sketches and dressed it in different outfits.

'I thought that his body and skin were very beautiful,' he would later say.

On occasion, Nilsen would place the corpse on his sofa, so that the two of them could watch television together.

Nilsen believed that he had killed a further ten or eleven young men in the Melrose Avenue flat. His murders started to follow a pattern: he would get the victim drunk, strangle him with a man's tie, take a bath with the body and then rape it. He later recalled how he felt on these occasions.

> 'The most exciting part was when I lifted a body and carried it. It was an expression of my power to have control. The dangling element of limp limbs was an expression of passivity. The more passive, the more powerful I was.'

The corpses were often kept for months. In each case, Nilsen would use his skills as a butcher to facilitate the inevitable disposal of the bodies. He would cut off the heads, remove the organs and dissect the torsos. In the evenings, he would put plastic bags containing entrails outside, to be eaten by scavenging animals.

On three occasions he built bonfires on a vacant piece of land, where he burned his victims' limbs. The neighbourhood children would gather around to watch the fire, but he quickly shooed them off.

Nilsen had several close calls at this time. In October of 1979, a young man named Andrew Ho told the police that Nilsen had attacked him, but he refused to provide a written statement or appear in court. Thirteen months later another man, Douglas Stewart, escaped from Nilsen's clutches, but Stewart's report to the police was dismissed as a spat between gay lovers. Nilsen left the Melrose Avenue flat for his Cranley Gardens attic rooms in October 1981. Although he continued killing, the new home provided some obstacles. At Melrose Avenue, Nilsen's butchered corpses could either be buried in the garden or on adjoining vacant land, but Cranley Gardens offered neither possibility.

Perhaps as a result, Nilsen killed only three men in his attic flat.

The first of them, John Howlett, had been particularly problematic. A former guardsman, he had fought strenuously when Nilsen had tried to strangle him, even though he was drunk. When Howlett became unconscious, Nilsen dragged the man to the bathtub and drowned him. He did not want to share his bed with Howlett's corpse so he cut it up, flushing the heart and lungs down the toilet. The head, hands, ribs and feet were boiled in a large pot on his kitchen stove.

Nilsen attempted to dispose of his victims' bodies by cutting them into manageable chunks and flushing them down the toilet, but it was a lengthy process. A backlog of corpses soon began to build up.

What the Dyno-Rod employee discovered on that February day in 1983 was the remains of Nilsen's second Cranley Gardens victim, 28-year-old Graham Allen.

After lifting up the drain's manhole cover, Michael Cattran was fairly certain that what he was seeing was human. However, the drain had been cleaned when he returned with his supervisor on the following day. When the police were called in they found a few small pieces of flesh. A laboratory analysis determined that they were indeed human. After questioning the other tenants, the police learned that Nilsen had been heard going up and down the stairs many times during the previous evening.

Smell of rotting flesh

What had been a busy day's work was not over yet – the suspect was due home from work. When Nilsen returned to 23 Cranley Gardens, he was met by Detective Chief Inspector Peter Jay. As the two men entered the attic flat, Jay immediately noticed the strong smell of rotting flesh. When he revealed that human remains had been found in the drains, Nilsen reacted with surprise. But Jay was having none of it.

'Don't mess about,' he told the young man, 'where's the rest of the body?'

Nilsen was taken aback. After a bit of hesitation he replied, 'In two plastic bags in the wardrobe next door.'

The civil servant was arrested and taken by car to the police station. During the brief ride, Jay turned to Nilsen and asked him a question.

'Are we talking about one body or two?' he said.

'Fifteen or sixteen,' was Nilsen's reply.

Nilsen's story sold papers. Although most of his victims had died at the Melrose Avenue flat in north London, he was dubbed the Muswell Hill Murderer. The press focused their attention on the grisly discoveries at Nilsen's Cranley Gardens flat.

The investigations at both addresses went on for months. It wasn't until 10 October 1983 that Nilsen's trial began. Facing six charges of murder and two of attempted murder, he pleaded diminished responsibility. The jury was torn on the issue, leading a judge, Mr Justice Croon-Johnson, to accept a majority verdict of guilty.

On 4 November 1983, Dennis Nilsen was handed a sentence of 25 years to life, but this was later amended by the Home Secretary, who wished to ensure that the murderer would never be released from prison.

Was the punishment enough?

On the eve of his trial, Nilsen wrote, 'I have judged myself more harshly than any court ever could.'

DAVID PARKER RAY AND CINDY HENDY

Truth or Consequences and the Trailer

Truth or Consequences, New Mexico was once a place of relaxation. The first people to enjoy its hospitality arrived over one hundred years ago. They were there to soak in the Geronimo Springs at John Cross Ranch. It would be the first of several dozen spas to be built around the heated groundwater that continues to bubble up in this city of less than 8,000 souls. The entire community was built around this natural phenomenon.

Anyone who wonders how important it once was to the local economy need look no further than the city's original name: Hot Springs. The city became Truth or Consequences in 1950, when the popular radio quiz show of that name offered to broadcast from the first community to rename itself after the show. It was all good fun.

The first indication of David Parker Ray's crimes came on 26 July 1996, when the sheriff's office in Truth or Consequences received a call from a young Marine. On the previous day he had argued with his wife Kelly Van Cleave and he had not seen or heard from her since. The anxious husband received only advice.

His wife had been gone such a short time that she could not be considered as a missing person. Based on past experience, the office had every reason to believe that Kelly would turn up.

Sure enough, the young man's wife returned home on the very next day. She had been brought back by an employee of nearby Elephant Butte State Park, where she had been found wandering in a dazed and incoherent state.

Kelly could account for only a few of the many hours she had been missing. After the fight with her husband, she remembered going to a friend's house. This was followed by trips to a number of bars, the last of which was the Blue Waters Saloon. It was there that Kelly ordered a beer, her first drink of the evening.

She soon began to feel dizzy. The sensation was not dissimilar to being drunk, but something was not quite right. Kelly could recall little else from this point onwards, though she was certain that an old friend, Jesse Ray, had offered to help. Those missing hours brought an end to Kelly's marriage. Her husband could never accept her disappearance, or her claim that she could not remember what had happened.

Nightmares

Jesse Ray might have been able to help… but she could not be found. Kelly soon left Truth or Consequences, never to return. She would never see Jesse again.

Now separated, Kelly began to suffer from nightmares. The horrifying images were remarkably consistent – she saw herself being tied to a table, being gagged with duct tape and having a knife held to her throat. Nothing quite made sense so Kelly never did report her strange experience to the authorities. All the sheriff's office at Truth or Consequences had on file was a seemingly trivial phone call from a distrusting husband. They could not have known that the woman who walked through their door on 7 July 1997 was bringing information that was related to Kelly's disappearance.

The woman had come to report that she had not heard from her 22-year-old daughter, Marie Parker, for several days. This time, there would be an investigation. In such a small city, it was not difficult to track the young woman's movements. Marie had last been seen on 5 July at the Blue Waters Saloon. She had been drinking with Jesse Ray. Jesse told the authorities that Marie had been drinking heavily so she had driven her home, but she had not seen her since.

But Jesse was not the only person that Marie had been drinking with on the night of her disappearance. Roy Yancy, an old boyfriend, had also been raising a glass at the Blue Waters Saloon. A Truth or Consequences boy born and raised, there was nothing in Roy's past to make the community proud.

As a child he had been part of a gang that had roamed Truth or Consequences strangling cats, poisoning dogs and tipping over gravestones, acts that led the city to cancel that year's

Hallowe'en festivities. He had also received a dishonourable discharge from the navy.

Marie might well have been in the company of an unsavoury character, but the Truth or Consequences sheriff's office saw nothing unusual about her disappearance. After all, the city was known for its transient population. They were all too ready to accept someone's hazy recollection of a girl accepting a ride out of the city. It was a typical story.

At around this time a new woman arrived in the small city. Cindy Hendy's history was anything but enviable. A victim of sexual abuse, she had been molested by her stepfather before being turned out on the street at the age of 11. Cindy had been a teenage mother, but only in the sense that she had given birth – other people had taken on the job of raising her daughter. When she arrived in Truth or Consequences, Cindy was on the run from a drugs charge. Several months earlier, she had supplied cocaine to an undercover agent. She was a violent woman with a short fuse, so it was not long before she found herself in the local jail. Days later she was sent out to Elephant Butte Lake on a work-release programme. It was there that she first met David Parker Ray, the father of her friend Jesse.

He was a quiet, though approachable and friendly man. Ray had been a neglected child. Unloved by his mother, his only real contact with his drifter father came in the form of periodic drunken visits. These invariably ended with the old man leaving behind a bag of pornographic magazines that portrayed sadomasochistic acts. His adult life was one of many marriages and many jobs. He had lived a transient life before 1984, when he settled down with his fourth wife in Elephant Butte. After acquiring a run-down bungalow on a little piece of property, Ray supported them by working as an aircraft engine repairman.

By 1995, his wife had left him. The fourth Mrs Ray would be the final Mrs Ray, but she was not his last companion. In January 1999, Cindy Hendy moved into Ray's bungalow. It mattered little that he was two decades older because the 38-year-old had met her soulmate – someone who, like herself, was obsessed with sadomasochistic sex.

Lonely newcomer

Cindy had been living with Ray for just one month when, on 16 February, she invited Angie Montano over for a visit. Angie, a single mother, was new to Truth or Consequences, and was eager to make friends. She had come to the wrong place, because she was blindfolded, strapped to a bed and sexually assaulted. Ray and Cindy's sadistic tastes went beyond rape. Angie was stunned by cattle prods and various other devices that Ray had made himself. After five days, Angie managed to get Ray to agree to her release. He drove her to the nearest highway and let her out. As luck would have it, she was picked up by a passing off-duty police officer. Angie shared her story with him, but she would not agree to making an official report. Just as Kelly Van Cleave had done four years earlier, Angie left Truth or Consequences, never to return.

Even as the assaults on Angie Montano were taking place, Cindy's mind was sometimes elsewhere. Though her 39th birthday had only just passed, she was about to become a grandmother. She made plans to attend the birth in her old home town of Monroe, Washington, but before she could go she needed to find a sex slave for Ray, someone who would meet his needs in her absence.

On 18 March, they drove through the streets of Albuquerque in Ray's motorhome, where they came upon Cynthia Vigil. She was a prostitute, so it was not difficult to get her into the vehicle, nor was it hard to overpower the 22-year-old. After being bound, Cynthia was taken back to the Elephant Butte bungalow, where she was collared, chained, blindfolded and gagged. A tape was then played to her. The voice was Ray's.

'Hello, bitch. Well, this tape's gettin' played again. Must mean I picked up another hooker. And I'll bet you wonder what the hell's goin' on here.'

Those were just the first few sentences in a recording that lasted over five minutes. Ray went on to describe how he and his 'lady friend' were going to rape and torture the listener.

'The gag is necessary,' he explained, 'because after a while you're goin' to be doin' a lot of screaming.'

True to the words of the tape, Ray and Cindy tortured and raped the prostitute over the course of the next three days. The assaults had no effect on Ray's work habits. As the fourth day began, he donned his state park uniform and drove off. Cindy was charged with keeping their victim under control. But his lady friend wasn't quite up to the task. In fact, she was downright sloppy.

When Cindy left the room to prepare a lunch of tuna sandwiches, the young prostitute noticed that her abductor had left behind the keys to her chains. After releasing herself, she grabbed the phone and called the Sierra County Sheriff's Office. Before she could say a word, Cindy was back in the room, bottle in hand. She took a violent swing at the prostitute, cutting her with the breaking glass. Cynthia noticed an ice pick while she was lying on the floor. She quickly grabbed it and stabbed her abductor in the back of the neck.

It was not a lethal blow, but it was enough to give Cynthia time to get out of the house. Naked except for a dog collar and chain, she ran out of the door and down the dusty, unpaved street. She was spotted by the drivers of two cars, but they just swerved to avoid the distressed, bleeding woman.

After about a mile, she came upon a trailer home. She burst through the door and fell at the feet of a woman watching television.

Scene of the crime

Just minutes after the first interrupted call, the Sierra County Sheriff's Office received a second one. When the authorities arrived at the mobile home they heard a horrific tale of torture and assault. As Cynthia Vigil was being transported to the local hospital, the sheriff's department decided to call in the state police.

Over a dozen officers converged on Ray's bungalow, only to find that Cindy had fled.

The house was a mess, with garbage littering the floor. If there was any order, it was found in Ray's instruments of torture, which were arranged on hooks hanging from the walls of several rooms. His library included books on Satanism, torture and violent pornography. There were also a number of medical books, which presumably enabled him to carry out many of his fantasies.

The hunt was now on for Ray and Cindy. The chase was as short as it was easy. The couple had not fled – instead, they were driving along the nearby roads, looking for their captive. Ray and Cindy were spotted within 15 minutes, a mere two blocks from their home. They quickly admitted that they had been looking for Cynthia Vigil, but they also came up with an implausible explanation for their actions. The abduction of the prostitute had been a humanitarian act, claimed Ray and Cindy. Her confinement had been nothing more than an effort to help the young woman kick her addiction to heroin.

The story fooled no one. Ray and Cindy were arrested and taken into custody. As the investigation of Ray's property began, the state law enforcement officials realized that they did not have the resources to deal with their discoveries. Lieutenant Richard Libicer of the New Mexico State Police explained the situation:

> *'I think it's safe to say that nothing that was inside that house was anything any of us had experienced before – or come across before – except maybe in a movie somewhere. It was just completely out of the realm of our experience.'*

The assortment of shackles and pulleys and other instruments of torture inside the bungalow appeared almost mundane compared to what was discovered inside a padlocked semi-trailer that was parked outside.

What Ray described as the 'Toy Box' contained hundreds of torture devices. Many of them, such as a machine that was used to electrocute women's breasts, had been designed and built by the former mechanic. At the centre of this horror was a gynaecology table. Cameras were installed, so that the women could see what was happening to them. Ray had also videotaped his assaults, including the one involving Kelly Van Cleave. She had supposedly been found wandering by a state park official – but the state park official was David Parker Ray.

The videotapes were a revelation. For a start, they linked Jesse Ray to her father's crimes. Kelly's evidence also proved useful, but the most damning testimony came from Cindy Hendy.

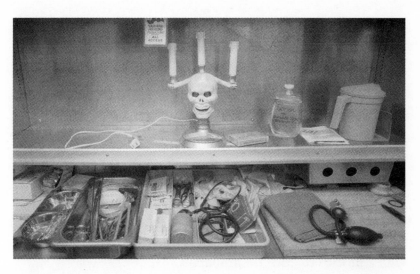

The 'Toy Box', a mobile torture chamber, was Ray's pride and joy – he put $100,000 into it

Within days of her arrest, the 39-year-old turned on her boyfriend. She told the investigators that Ray had been abducting and torturing women for many years. What is more, Ray had told Cindy that his fantasies had often ended in murder.

Subsequent searches of Elephant Butte Lake and the surrounding countryside revealed nothing, but the police remain convinced that Ray had killed at least one person. Cindy also confirmed that Jesse had participated in at least some of the abductions. She added that she often worked in tandem with Roy Yancy.

Soft centre

Despite his tough demeanour, Roy caved in when he was arrested. He told the police that he and Jesse had drugged Marie Parker, the young woman who had gone missing three years earlier. They had taken her to Elephant Butte, where she was tortured. When Ray tired of her, he instructed Roy to kill the woman who had once been his girlfriend.

The body was never found.

Roy Yancy pleaded guilty to second-degree murder and was sentenced to 20 years in prison.

After pleading guilty to kidnapping Kelly Van Cleave and Marie Parker, Jesse Ray received a nine-year sentence.

Facing the possibility of 197 years in prison, Cindy Hendy made a deal with the prosecutors. After pleading guilty to her crimes against Cynthia Vigil she received a 36-year sentence, with a further 18 years on probation.

Even Ray appeared to co-operate with the authorities, but only to the extent of describing his fantasies. He denied that he had abducted or murdered anyone. Any sadomasochistic activities had been between consenting adults. 'I got pleasure out of the woman getting pleasure,' he told one investigator. 'I did what they wanted me to do.'

Ray faced three trials for his crimes against Kelly Van Cleave, Cynthia Vigil and Angie Montano. He was found guilty in the first trial, but part of the way through the second he too made a deal. Ray agreed to plead guilty in exchange for Jesse's release. The case concerning Angie Montano was never heard because she had died of cancer.

On 30 September 2001, David Parker Ray received a 224-year sentence for his crimes against Kelly Van Cleave and Cynthia Vigil. In the end, Ray did not serve so much as a year. On 28 May 2002 he slumped over in a holding cell, killed by a massive heart attack.

'Satan has a place for you. I hope you burn in hell forever,' Cynthia Vigil's grandmother had once yelled at him.

One wonders whether the words meant anything to Ray. The one sign he had put up in his 'Toy Box' read: 'SATAN'S DEN'.

WOLFGANG PRIKLOPIL
A New Use for an Old Bomb Shelter

On 8 September 2006, a quiet funeral was held in the town of Laxenburg, just to the south of Vienna. The deceased, a youngish-looking 44-year-old named Wolfgang Priklopil, had committed suicide 16 days earlier. His death was front page news in Austria, because he had become notorious for holding a girl captive for more than eight years without anyone's knowledge. It was a story that had horrified a nation, yet among those who mourned Wolfgang was the very girl he had kidnapped.

Curiously ordinary

Wolfgang's curious life began in Hainburg an der Donau, a small Austrian town on the Danube, within sight of Slovakia.

*Wolfgang Priklopil was a courteous and obedient child, who loved
playing with model trains*

The Priklopils were comfortably off, though far from wealthy. Wolfgang's father, Karl, was a cognac salesman and Waltraud, his mother, worked in a shoe shop. An only child, he enjoyed travelling to Italy, Germany and rural Austria with his parents, but otherwise he was very much a loner. Wolfgang had no real friends, but that did not trouble him. His happiest moments were spent alone in his room, reading, working on jigsaw puzzles and playing with his model trains. He was an average student, though his school records indicate that he did shine in one area: he was a courteous and obedient child.

In 1972, the year of Wolfgang's 10th birthday, the Priklopil family moved to number 60 Heinestrasse in the Vienna suburb of Strasshof. Karl had inherited the property after the death of his father. It was an unremarkable house, except for one feature. In the 1950s an illicit bomb shelter had been built off the cellar. In the absence of a nuclear holocaust, the five square-metre room (54 square feet) had seen a number of different uses over the years, including a playroom where young Wolfgang operated his model trains.

Wolfgang left school at the age of 15 to become an apprentice at Siemens. His good work eventually earned him a position within the firm. Although he was a young man with a good income, he showed no interest in dating and socializing and he continued to live with his parents.

Even though he was not blessed with movie-star good looks, his appearance was pleasant enough. He had a boyish face and a slim build and he always seemed younger than his years – yet Wolfgang was unhappy and insecure about his looks. His worst feature, he thought, was his nose. For a time, he considered plastic surgery.

When Karl died of bowel cancer in 1986, Waltraud moved back to the apartment that they had left 15 years earlier. Wolfgang stayed on at 60 Heinestrasse for a time, but he eventually joined his mother.

Several more years would pass before he finally made a move towards independence. At 31, he moved back to 60 Heinestrasse, but he returned to his mother's flat at weekends. For her part, Waltraud continued to nurture her son by supplying him with frozen home-cooked meals.

Invitation

It was during this slow move towards independence that an old Siemens colleague, Ernst Holzapfel, invited Wolfgang to join him in a construction, renovation and interior decoration business. The venture was an immediate success, which gave Wolfgang the money and the time to follow his dream, which was kidnapping a young girl.

Over a period of months, he converted the old bomb shelter into something resembling a jail cell.

A toilet and a sink were installed and insulation of the type used in recording studios made it all soundproof. To maintain secrecy, Wolfgang performed every stage of the work by himself.

On 2 March 1998, at the age of 35, Wolfgang found the girl of his dreams.

He abducted Natascha Kampusch as she was walking through the rain to school. Wolfgang simply stopped his Mercedes van, grabbed her around the waist and drove away. At the Heinestrasse house, Natascha was introduced to the windowless room that would be her home for the remaining years of her childhood.

For all his planning, Wolfgang did not know what to do

with his captive at first. Natascha had seen news reports about paedophiles, so she feared that she was going to be molested.

'Are you going to molest me?' she asked.

'You're too young for that. I'd never do that,' Wolfgang replied.

As the days passed, fear was replaced by boredom, because Natascha spent nearly all of her time alone. The only break in her routine came when Wolfgang arrived with food, which they shared at a folding table.

The only time physical contact was made was when he methodically washed Natascha in the sink – in her words, 'He scrubbed me down as if I were a car.'

Locked away

During her first six months in captivity, she did not once leave the old bomb shelter. Her first foray into the world outside the cramped concrete room came when Wolfgang unexpectedly agreed that she could have a bath. As he led Natascha through the unfamiliar house, Wolfgang uttered a sinister warning.

'All the windows and exits have been secured with explosive devices – if you open a window, you'll blow yourself up.'

The threat was uncharacteristic, because for the first year or so Wolfgang acted dispassionately. However, his behaviour underwent a radical change when Natascha entered puberty at the age of 12.

Without any reason, he started to kick and punch her. Even more disturbing, Wolfgang also began what Natascha describes as 'minor sexual assaults'.

'You are no longer Natascha,' he said. 'You now belong to me.' Wolfgang forced her to choose a new name for herself. For the next seven years, she would be known as 'Bibiane'.

The old bomb shelter which became Natascha's prison cell for 3,096 days

In order to reinforce his claim on the girl's life, Wolfgang rigged up an intercom, into which he would repeat in a monotone: 'Obey! Obey! Obey!'

Increasingly, she was brought upstairs to do housework. She would also be manacled and made to lie next to Wolfgang as he slept.

When Natascha was 15, Wolfgang began taking her out of the house. Though she was anything but free, for the first time in years she felt the sun, breathed fresh air and saw something of the world beyond her abductor's house. Wolfgang took her shopping and they went for drives. When the neighbours were not around, they even went swimming in the pool next door.

This all-too-brief exposure to the normal, outside world gave Natascha hope. In her biography, she writes, 'I was immeasurably grateful to the kidnapper for such small pleasures. I still am.'

Although the excursions initially had a positive effect on Natascha, the benefits diminished over the years. By the time she was 16, she had become severely depressed.

Wolfgang often had to force his captive out of her dungeon. She became weak with hunger, yet she would not eat. Hours were spent crying while she lay curled up in a foetal position. Wolfgang tried to instil hope in her by describing a 'life together' in which she would have more freedom. Often, he would tell Natascha these things as she lay manacled beside him in bed.

Despite her depression, the outings continued. Years later Natascha recalled a visit to a hardware store, during which she was tempted to expose her captor. But when she looked at the other men milling around her, they started to look unfriendly and hostile. On one memorable occasion, the two travelled to Vienna for a skiing holiday. What was meant to be a celebration of Natascha's 18th birthday got off to a bad start. While he was planning the trip, Wolfgang became annoyed at the great amount of money he would spend.

'You're only exploiting my benevolence!' he yelled. 'You're nothing without me. Nothing!'

In turn Natascha lost her temper, telling Wolfgang that she refused to go on the ski trip. That was too much for her captor. After all, she was in no position to refuse any of his requests. Wolfgang grabbed a crowbar and slammed it against her upper thigh. Natascha would ski in Vienna whether she liked it or not.

Bizarre situation

Now that she was 18, the little girl was now legally a woman. She no longer suffered from the depression that had crippled her just two years earlier. As she became bolder, she confronted Wolfgang about the bizarre situation that he had created. One day, she told her captor, it would have to come to an end. She even advised Wolfgang to kill himself.

'You won't be able to find any other way out anyway,' Natascha said. She then added something that just might have given him ideas. 'Don't worry,' she told him. 'If I run away, I'll throw myself in front of a train. I'd never put you in any danger.'

On the morning of 23 August 2006, three weeks after uttering those words, Natascha finally escaped. Her move towards freedom was not quite spontaneous. She had been turning the idea over in her mind. Wolfgang had ordered Natascha to clean the van in which she had been abducted eight and a half years earlier. When his mobile phone rang, he became distracted, walking away from the vehicle as he engaged in conversation.

There had been other escape opportunities, but Natascha only chose to take this one.

She sprinted towards the gate that led to the street, threw it open and ran for her life. After 3,096 days Natascha Kampusch was free.

Running through the streets, she asked the first people she saw – two adults and a child – to telephone the police, but they had no mobile. Ringing the doorbell of the first house she came to also brought no response. At another house she was met by a distrustful elderly woman, who made her wait outside as she called the police.

Natascha was taken to the police station at Deutsch-Wagram. Her incredible story was met with scepticism by some of the officers, but this quickly faded. In the afternoon she learned that the police were hunting for Wolfgang.

Suicide

Despite what she had told her captor three weeks earlier, Natascha had not jumped in front of a train, nor was she planning to do so. However, she did expect Wolfgang to take his life.

At one minute to nine in the evening, Wolfgang stepped in front of a moving train outside Vienna's northern railway station.

Natascha was gradually introduced to the glare of publicity. Guided by a media adviser, she gave several television interviews, but she did not give much away. In particular, she refused to discuss any 'personal or intimate details'. But surely Wolfgang had raped the girl… or had he? No one quite knew what to make of her mourning his death?

In 2010 it was revealed that just before he died Wolfgang told his partner, Ernst Holzapfel, that he had intended to adopt a new identity as a Czech. His plan had been to begin life anew with Natascha as his virgin bride.

Today, Natascha owns the house in which she was held captive. She has said that she carries a photograph of Priklopil, a man she describes as a 'paranoid psychopath', with her at all times.

JOHN EDWARD ROBINSON

The Slavemaster's Storage Locker

John Edward Robinson used many pseudonyms, but his best-known alias was perhaps 'the Slavemaster', the name he used when he roamed around the online chat rooms that were frequented by those interested in bondage, discipline and the sadomasochistic lifestyle. It was in many ways a tight community. Many of its members were looking for a bondage relationship of some sort. Robinson, however, was not interested in fulfilling the desires of others. He had his own personal agenda.

Robinson was born on 27 December 1943 in Cicero, Illinois, a town that was made famous by its connection with Al Capone,

As a boy, Robinson had found comfort in religion as an escape from the harsh life at home

the notorious Chicago gangster. He was the third of five children in a working-class family that was weakened by an alcoholic father. Perhaps his disciplinarian mother was trying to make up for her husband's failings. Whatever the case, Robinson's early life was not enviable. Fortunately, he found a certain amount of solace in the Catholic Church.

Conman and serial killer

If Robinson had any devout thoughts as a boy, they were left far behind him when he became a conman and a serial killer. Innumerable lies would fall from his lips, but some very improbable stories from his past were actually true. For example, he really had sung in front of Queen Elizabeth at the famous London Palladium. This episode had taken place in November 1957, when he was on a European tour with a troop of Eagle Scouts. Backstage, he had even received a kiss from Judy Garland.

Robinson's stage appearance suggests that he was an outgoing sort of a boy, but that was not the case. In fact he was quiet and reserved, someone who preferred solitude and study.

Decades later, his fellow Eagle Scouts would recall that he had intended to become a priest. Indeed, he had said as much to Gracie Fields, whom he had met at the Palladium. Robinson told those gathered backstage that one day he hoped to be assigned to work at the Vatican.

At that point he was telling the truth. When he returned from the Eagle Scout tour, he began to study at Chicago's Archbishop Quigley Preparatory Seminary. Unfortunately, the studious boy turned out to be not such a good student.

Frustrated, he began lashing out at his classmates, both

verbally and physically. His antics resulted in frequent detentions and he was expelled at the end of his first year.

Fresh start

Looking for another career path, in 1961 he entered Morton Junior College, not far from his home in Cicero, where he began training to become an X-ray technician. Though he considered his entry to the college as the first step in a path that would lead to medical school, Robinson again struggled.

Less than two years later, he left Morton College without obtaining a certificate.

A fresh start was needed, he thought, so in 1964 he moved to Kansas City, where he married a young woman named Nancy Jo Lynch. It was at about this time that the former seminary student committed his first known crime. Using fake diplomas and forged letters of recommendation, he obtained a position as an X-ray technician at the city's Children's Mercy Hospital. Robinson's fraud was soon exposed. However, through his own incompetence, it became clear to fellow medical employees that he was not a certified technician. What is more, he did not appear to have the skill or the intelligence to become one.

In 1965, shortly after the birth of his first child, Robinson's fraud was exposed and he was quietly dismissed by the hospital. Undisturbed by an experience that could and should have involved criminal charges, Robinson continued to present himself as a certified X-ray technician. The deceit was just one element in a young life that had come to be filled with lies. While Nancy Jo stayed at home caring for their son, also called John, Robinson ran around with other women.

In 1966, aged 22, he presented his false documents to Dr

Wallace Graham, former physician to President Harry Truman. Impressed by Robinson's credentials and the story about having performed for the queen of England, Graham gave the young man a good position in his business, the Fountain Plaza X-ray Laboratory. Within two years, Robinson had turned the thriving, professional business on its head. He had sex with the staff, he had sex with the patients and he nearly bankrupted the clinic by stealing approximately $200,000 from its accounts. His escapades came to a halt in 1969, when he was led away from the laboratory in handcuffs.

False credentials

Despite his false credentials, Robinson was charged only with embezzlement. In court he presented himself as a remorseful young man and he promised that he would make restitution. As a reward for his convincing performance, he received three years' probation instead of jail time. Robinson was not really remorseful and he had learned no lessons. Months into his probation, he was arrested for stealing over 6,000 postage stamps from his new employer, Mobil Oil. He managed to avoid being sent to prison by once again agreeing to return the money.

Now out of work, Robinson relocated his family to Chicago, where he accepted a job selling insurance for R.B. Jones. He kept the move secret because it was a clear violation of his probation.

For once, the 26-year-old man proved invaluable to his employer because he was one of the firm's finest salesmen. It therefore came as a surprise to the firm's management when he was caught embezzling nearly $6,000.

For the third time in less than three years, Robinson appeared in court as a seemingly remorseful man. Again, he offered to pay restitution and again the charges were dropped. No doubt the court felt some sympathy for poor Mrs Robinson, who was many months pregnant with twins at the time. However, the incident had exposed Robinson's parole violation, so he was forced to move his growing family back to Kansas City. His parole was extended by a further three years, but this had no effect on his behaviour. Though he had no qualifications, he established Professional Services Association, Inc., a medical consulting business. Using still more forged documents, he was hired by a number of organizations and he won a large contract from the University of Kansas Medical Center.

Community-minded

When he was not working at his fraudulent business or visiting the probation officer, Robinson cultivated a reputation as a good community-minded family man. He coached basketball and T-ball, taught Sunday school, became a scoutmaster and played Santa Claus at children's Christmas parties. In 1975, when a Federal Grand Jury indicted Robinson for mail fraud, securities fraud and misrepresenting his medical consulting firm, no one noticed. A few months later, he was fined $2,500 after pleading guilty to an interstate securities fraud.

Robinson's probation was extended yet again, but it did not appear to faze the man. And that $2,500 fine? He hardly noticed it. The scoutmaster was making a large income from his illegal business dealings.

All of this wealth enabled the Robinsons to move into a larger home. They also bought a couple of horses and took vacations. Some of this luxury was paid for by someone he had conned out of $25,000. The man thought he was investing in a company called Hydro-Gro. A further few thousand dollars came in when he presented himself as a divorce attorney to a woman 'client'. In nearly every case, his victims were too embarrassed to report his crimes to the authorities.

Despite all of this illegal activity, Robinson's reputation in Kansas City remained untarnished until 1977, when his ego got the better of him. It all began when he managed to charm his way on to the board of a local charitable organization.

He then sent out a number of invitations to a luncheon in honour of a yet-to-be-announced 'Kansas City Man of the Year'. When his name was read out, Robinson showed great surprise. Then with a certain degree of humility he accepted the award from the state senator. The scam was exposed two weeks later in an article published in *The Kansas City Star*. Nancy Jo Robinson and the children did not dare show their faces in public, but John Edward Robinson, on the other hand, appeared to be completely undaunted.

Robinson's probation was finally lifted in 1979, after almost a decade. His probation officer gave him a glowing report. That same year, Robinson was hired by a grocery chain as employee relations manager. He soon began an affair with his secretary and with her help he managed to embezzle thousands of dollars by cashing cheques for non-existent employees. After he was caught, he paid $50,000 in restitution.

This had been Robinson's biggest known scam, yet he still managed to avoid a prison sentence. A year later, however, his luck ran out when he was handed a 60-day jail sentence for stealing a $6,000 cheque. He was unrepentant and unchanged when he emerged from prison and he was immediately on the lookout for more victims – only he was now prepared to take more than just their money.

It is almost certain that Robinson murdered for the first time in 1984. His victim was a 19-year-old named Paula Godfrey. He had hired her as a sales representative for Equi-Plus and Equi-2, his two latest scam companies. That September, Paula told her family and friends that she was being sent away to a training seminar. The last anyone saw of her was when Robinson picked her up, ostensibly to drive her to the airport. Several days later, her parents received a typewritten letter bearing her signature, in which she stated that she never wanted to see them again. She also thanked Robinson for his help. Paula Godfrey's disappearance remains a mystery to this day.

The Slavemaster

Paula's parents did not know that Equi-Plus and Equi-2 were covers. It is highly likely that Paula herself did not know either. They were false companies, it is true, but there was also a business going on underneath it all. Using the company names, Robinson rented a duplex in which he set up a brothel that specialized in sadomasochism. Robinson shared his clients' taste for rough sex. In fact, he had become a high-standing person in a secretive cult that called itself the International Council of Masters. He was known as 'the Slavemaster'.

Shortly after saleswoman Paula Godfrey vanished, Robinson saw an opportunity to make some quick and easy money. His younger brother Don and Don's wife Helen, a childless couple, had spent many unsuccessful years attempting to adopt a baby. Then one day Robinson told them of a lawyer friend who specialized in such matters. Don gave his brother $2,500 to be paid to the imaginary attorney. Months passed, but there was no baby.

Robinson provided all sorts of excuses, all purporting to come from the non-existent lawyer. In reality, he had been frustrated in his attempts to buy a child on the black market. Finally, at the beginning of 1985, he came across 19-year-old Lisa Stasi and her 4-month-old baby daughter Tiffany in a Kansas City battered women's shelter. The young mother's life had been hard after she had become estranged from her husband.

Passing himself off as 'John Osborne', a children's aid worker, Robinson painted a colourful portrait of a programme that would provide the teenager with housing, job training, day care and a monthly cheque of $800. The only downside was that Lisa would have to spend a few months in Texas, where she would be trained to work as a silkscreen printer.

On 9 January, 'Osborne' picked up the mother and child. The next day, her mother-in-law received a phone call in which a panicked Lisa said that an unidentified 'they' had declared that she was an unfit mother. They were about to seize her baby.

'Here they come!' Lisa exclaimed. Then the line went dead.

She was never heard from again, except for a typewritten letter to her mother-in-law in which she said that she wanted to move on with her life. But Lisa Stasi could not type.

On 12 January, Don and Helen Robinson welcomed a beautiful four-month-old baby girl to their family. John Robinson was given an additional $3,000 to pass on to his imaginary lawyer friend. The disguise of 'John Osborne' was easily penetrated, however. The authorities soon linked Robinson to Lisa's disappearance and they also connected his name with the Paula Godfrey case. An FBI unit was put on his tail. Despite this ongoing investigation

Catherine Clampitt, another of his employees, vanished in June 1987.

At about the same time, successful businessman John Robinson appeared on the cover of *Farm Journal*. The national magazine encouraged farmers to invest their money in Equi-Plus and Equi-2. Robinson might have managed to get away with Catherine Clampitt's murder, and he certainly managed to cheat a few farmers out of their savings, but 1987 was not a good year for the Slavemaster. Convicted on numerous counts of fraud, he was handed down a 14-year sentence. Without his guidance, his businesses quickly collapsed. The Robinson family lost their luxurious home and ended up in a trailer park outside the city of Olathe, where Nancy Jo got a job as manager.

Banged up

As a guest of the State of Missouri, Robinson was shuffled from prison to prison, but he served less than four years in total. His last and longest stay was at the Western Missouri Correctional Facility, where he met an attractive 49-year-old named Beverly Bonner, the prison librarian. Beverly soon fell for Robinson's charm. In 1993, not long after he was released on parole, she divorced her husband, a prison doctor, and went to work in a business that Robinson had supposedly set up in Olathe. There is no evidence whatsoever that Beverly Bonner lived more than a day in her adopted city. Yet, her devoted ex-husband was prompt with his alimony cheques, which Robinson summarily cashed.

Beverly's mother and ex-husband thought she was travelling the world on business. The staff of a Raymore, Missouri storage facility believed her to be in Australia, likely never to return. They'd been told this by her employer and friend John Robinson, who had rented out a locker for her belongings. Beverly was having such a good time Down Under, he had said, that 'she would probably never come back'.

In fact, Beverly was very close by. Her body was slowly decomposing in a sealed drum that sat next to all her belongings. There were two other drums in the rented storage room, both of which held corpses.

Anyone opening the first container would have found the body of 45-year-old Sheila Faith. The drum next to hers contained the body of her daughter Debbie, a 15-year-old who had suffered from spina bifida. Sheila was a widow who had lived much of her rather challenging life in Fullerton, California. She was a lonely woman who had sought friendship and companionship through online chat rooms.

Though she had been through a run of bad experiences, in the summer of 1994, Sheila thought she had found someone with whom she might spend the rest of her life. 'John' was wealthy and generous. He was not only going to support her but he would also pay for Debbie's therapy. And he would give her a job into the bargain.

Within a matter of weeks Sheila and Debbie moved to Kansas City. Only hours later, they had disappeared. No one noticed that the mother and her daughter had gone missing because they had no real family. With no one the wiser, 'John' – that is, John Robinson – cashed the first of the monthly disability cheques that were being forwarded from California. He would do that for the next seven years.

In 1994, most Americans had never used the Internet, but Robinson was an early adopter. He immediately saw it as a way of hooking up with others who shared his uncommon sexual tastes. The advent of the personal computer and the Internet brought with it other benefits. Because of his criminal record Robinson was prevented from establishing a new company, but that did not stop him from setting up a magazine for trailer park residents. The new periodical did not take too much putting together when Robinson employed his new-found computing skills. It was virtually identical to an existing Kansas City magazine. Understandably, the rival magazine's proprietors threatened Robinson with a lawsuit, but he paid them no heed.

Back home in the trailer park that Nancy Jo managed, he settled into a pleasant routine that involved cashing cheques sent to Beverly and Sheila and trawling chat rooms.

Hidden mistress

Though he kept a mistress hidden away in a Kansas City apartment, Robinson was always keeping an eye out for women who were interested in bondage and sadomasochism.

In 1997, he found one in a 21-year-old Polish immigrant named Izabela Lewicka, who was living in Indiana with her university professor parents. A fine arts student with a love of bondage and the gothic, she moved to be with Robinson in Kansas City. She willingly signed a 115-item contract giving him complete control over every aspect of her life, in return for the sex that she craved.

By 1998, Robinson's bondage partner was calling herself Izabela Lewicka Robinson. One day she accompanied Robinson to the local registrar's office, where they applied for a marriage licence. Although Izabela did not know it, he was still married to Nancy Jo, so the girl's 54-year-old 'fiancé' never bothered to pick the licence up. After telling friends that she was about to go on a long trip with Robinson, Izabela disappeared, along with all of the money in her various bank accounts. Robinson told someone who enquired after her that she had been deported for smoking marijuana.

Even while he was lording over Izabela as the Slavemaster, Robinson was chatting online with Suzette Trouten, a 27-year-old nursing assistant who lived in Newport, Michigan. She was offered an appealing new life by her online friend. Her days would be spent taking care of Robinson's diabetic wheelchair-bound father, while her nights would be spent living out her fantasies as a sex slave. What the poor woman didn't know is that the Slavemaster's father had died ten years earlier.

In February 2000, Suzette arrived at Robinson's home – not the trailer in which he lived with Nancy Jo, but a 16-acre farm an hour to the south in La Cygne, Kansas. Robinson – or, as she knew him, 'J.R. Turner' – had bought the property in the previous September.

Suzette's friends – and she had many – never heard from her again after she reached Kansas.

It seemed very strange to them – she had never let so much as a day pass by without telephoning, emailing or chatting online.

Her mother, Carolyn, with whom she had been living, was particularly disturbed. Soon letters began arriving, but these only served to raise suspicion that something was amiss. They were typed – and Suzette never typed. Also the spelling was flawless – and Suzette was a notoriously poor speller. Most disconcerting of all was the fact that Suzette wrote that she was travelling abroad, yet the postmarks all indicated Kansas City.

When Carolyn tried the telephone number that Suzette had left, she was surprised to find herself speaking to the man who called himself 'J.R. Turner'. After all, he was supposedly travelling with her daughter. Robinson explained that Suzette had stolen some money from him and had run off with an acquaintance. For Carolyn, this was too much to be believed. After hanging up on Robinson, she telephoned the police. In doing so, she handed the authorities a gift. They had already increased their surveillance of Robinson and his properties, but the new information that Carolyn had supplied was enough to justify a wiretap and allow them to monitor his online activities.

They discovered that Robinson was in contact with dozens of women, but was increasingly focusing on just one: Sally Russell, an unemployed psychologist. On Easter weekend 2000, when she left her Texas home to meet Robinson in a Kansas motel room, detectives were listening in from the next room. The two engaged in rough sex and it appeared that the Slavemaster made the psychiatrist perform various sex acts against her wishes. When he was through, Robinson took her possessions and her money, leaving her to find her own way home.

A second woman from Texas, an accountant named Jeanna, was treated similarly, but with one significant difference – Robinson ordered her to pack up all her belongings and return to him. This she did, but after a particularly violent sexual encounter she became frightened and contacted the police.

As the county prosecutor and the police considered the next move, they learned that Robinson had seduced another woman, Vickie, through the Internet. She was preparing to leave her Tennessee home with her 8-year-old daughter for a life of servitude at the La Cygne farm.

There was no way that they were going to let the Slavemaster near a small girl. The authorities convinced her to file a complaint of sexual battery against Robinson. A second complaint, the theft of her sex toys – valued at roughly $700 – helped secure a search warrant.

On 2 June 2000, Robinson was arrested. Police investigators then began searching his properties and the rented storage lockers. Izabela and Suzette's bodies were found in sealed 55-gallon drums on the farm and shortly afterwards the bodies of Beverly Bonner and Sheila and Debbie Faith were also discovered.

All were in an advanced state of decomposition – their corpses were sitting in a putrid pool of what had once been body fat.

In the storage locker the drums had begun to leak. Robinson had scattered cat litter on the concrete floor in a fairly amateurish effort to absorb as much of the bodily fluids as possible. Identification was only made possible with the aid of dental records.

Although the authorities were absolutely certain that Robinson had murdered Paula Godfrey, Lisa Stasi and Catherine Clampitt, their bodies were never found.

Robinson's crimes, together with the titillating and shocking details of his deviant sex life, became fodder for the local media. His family retreated, eventually issuing a brief statement:

'While we do not discount the information that has and continues to come to light, we do not know the person whom we have read and heard about on TV. The John Robinson we know has always been a loving and caring father.'

A loving and caring father, perhaps, but John Edward Robinson had been an abusive husband.

Not only had he been unfaithful but for decades he had also been beating his wife. Then there was the underlying implication that Robinson had been an upstanding person, something very much at odds with his lengthy criminal record.

As new details came to light, the media came up with a neat label for Robinson. He became famous as 'the first Internet serial killer'. His arrest resulted in a tug of war between the two states in which he had committed his murders. In the end, Robinson was tried only in Missouri, where he faced murder charges relating to the deaths of Izabela, Suzette and Lisa.

On 21 January 2003, John Edward Robinson was found guilty of murdering all three women. He was sentenced to two penalties of death and one of life imprisonment.

The Eagle Scout who once sang for the queen of England moved on to Death Row in the El Dorado Correctional Facility in Wichita, Kansas, and in 2005 his wife filed for divorce.

MICHAEL RYAN
The Archangel's Hog Shed

Michael Ryan was always keen to share his violent fantasies. At social gatherings he would often go on about being a Mafia hitman or a CIA operative. Not that this overweight truck driver was either, mind you: it was just that he wanted to be like those people. Ryan dreamed of blowing up buildings or becoming an assassin, but in the end he killed no one. Instead, he got other people to do it for him.

There was really nothing in Michael Ryan's background that would have appealed to the CIA recruiters. He was a high school drop-out, he had a violent temper, he liked to get into fights and he was a regular marijuana user. On top of all that, he also had a fondness for drink, though this did not prevent him from becoming a truck driver.

Ryan prepared for the coming battle between good and evil with military-type drills and practice

One victim of Ryan's violent behaviour was his wife Ruth. They got married in 1968, a few months after his 20th birthday. Ruth was small and slight, so she was no match for her husband, who stood 6 ft 2 in tall and weighed 220 lbs (100 kg). Dennis, their only child, was also a recipient of Ryan's kicks and punches.

Then, one evening in May 1982, Ryan found God.

This momentous meeting took place during a lecture given by the Reverend James Wickstrom in Hiawatha, Kansas. The pastor's words were unlike anything Ryan had ever heard in the Baptist church of his youth. Wickstrom told his audience that Anglo-Saxons were the true Israelites, that Jews controlled the banks and that a day of reckoning was on the horizon. Invoking the ancient name for God, he declared: 'Yahweh is a god of war! He came not in peace, but to send a sword.'

'Remember,' the pastor told the crowd, 'Yahweh said it's okay to kill, but thou shalt not murder. You must kill the enemy of Yahweh – that is dictated!'

Indoctrination

Ryan heard more than talk about religion that evening. Wickstrom was one of the leading figures in a group dedicated to the 'return of white Anglo-Saxon Christians to the rightful control of America'. The Posse Comitatus, as they called themselves, railed against the state and the federal government because they believed that government should only exist at the county level. These beliefs were tied up with Wickstrom's interpretations of the Bible.

After the talk, Ryan met Wickstrom for the first time. It was a brief encounter, but it made a big impression. 'You are a true

Israelite!' the preacher exclaimed. Six months passed before the two men met again. This time, the location – a Best Western motel room – was much more intimate. It was there that Wickstrom convinced Ryan that he possessed the ability – or the 'power' – to receive advice from God on all daily matters, no matter how trivial and seemingly inconsequential.

Driving home after the meeting, Ryan was like a man possessed.

'This is one of the most important things to happen in my life,' he told his brother-in-law Steve Patterson. 'I am beginning to see why I need to be here in this life.'

Over the following months, Ryan immersed himself in Wickstrom's teachings. He listened to cassette tapes of the cleric's sermons and he studied his pamphlets.

Ryan also attended Bible meetings hosted by Posse Comitatus members, but he came away disappointed. It seemed that the farming families who had opened up their homes were more interested in discussing taxes, agricultural policy and politics than Yahweh as a god of war.

The Battle of Armageddon, mankind's final epic struggle, became Ryan's focus. With great conviction, he argued that the event would take place in Kansas.

It was all a bit much, even for those who followed the teachings of the Reverend Wickstrom. People also grew tired of Ryan's constant bragging. He would go on and on about having lost two toes while serving with the Green Berets in Vietnam, when in reality every day of his 34 years had been spent in the United States. It was true that Ryan had *tried* to join the army, but he had been turned down on medical grounds. And those two missing toes? They were the result of a self-inflicted wound, an accident that had taken place when Ryan had discharged a rifle in the back of his grandfather's pick-up truck.

But some people were taken in by Ryan's lies about life as a Green Beret. Hog breeder Jimmy Haverkamp was one of them. Haverkamp had renounced his Catholic upbringing to follow the Reverend Wickstrom and he would also become Ryan's first follower. The hog breeder was soon joined by other converts, including recently-widowed farmer Rick Stice. Heavily in debt and facing bankruptcy, Stice was attracted by the anti-government rhetoric of the Posse Comitatus and he was very impressed by Ryan's closeness to Wickstrom. The three men even visited the minister in his modest home, after which Michael Ryan told them that his Christian name was no accident – he was the very embodiment of the archangel Michael, the field commander in the Army of God.

Ryan and his followers prepared for the coming conflict by robbing banks. Money was required to construct the bunker from which the Battle of Armageddon would be fought. As the months went by, Ryan gradually began to distance himself from Wickstrom. Eventually, he severed ties with the Posse Comitatus. Its founder was devoting too much of his time to politics and not enough to Yahweh. By early 1984 Ryan had over a dozen followers, including Haverkamp's sister Cheryl, whom he had taken as a second wife. The group moved on to the 80-acre Stice farm, just outside the small, isolated village of Rulo in the southeast corner of Nebraska. It was here that Ryan's male followers would prepare for the coming battle between good and evil.

Ryan staged military-type drills and stockpiled weapons, much to the distress of the neighbouring farmers. They complained to the authorities in vain – as far as anyone could tell, Ryan and his followers were breaking no laws. But this was still Stice's farm. The hog farmer had not been sure about allowing Ryan to use his land, but he had eventually agreed to his leader's request. Now he was beginning to regret his decision. The situation was made all the more tense by the fact that Stice's youngest son Luke despised Ryan. In turn, Ryan declared that the 5-year-old was 'of Satan'.

Things would only get worse for Stice. Only months earlier, Ryan had blessed the marriage of Stice and his new wife Lisa, but now he was trying to tear them apart. As 1984 came to a close, Ryan took Lisa to Kansas City, where he told her that Yahweh had decreed that she should leave her husband and become one of his wives. It did not matter that she was pregnant, because the unborn child was not Stice's – it was the result of an immaculate conception. Convinced that her role had been ordained by Yahweh, Lisa put up no resistance.

Shortly afterwards, Ryan announced that Yahweh had given him a gift of slaves – Stice and his son Luke. There was a third slave, a former hardware store employee named James Thimm. Just days before, Ryan's 26-year-old follower had dared to question his leader's policies. After listening to Thimm's hesitant words, Ryan became livid.

'You need to get the f**k out of here if you're talkin' like that! Yahweh doesn't want Satan's people on this farm, bud, you're a proselyte! There's only one place for you... that's in hell. You better think about leaving!'

That last suggestion was the best advice Ryan ever gave the young man, but he did not take it. Now it was too late.

Luke was the first person to suffer at Ryan's hands. He beat the boy, stripped off his clothing and made him roll around in the cold February snow. Then he made him put a pistol in his mouth and pull the trigger. It was empty.

After that, Ryan shot the boy in the arm, claiming that it was Yahweh who had pulled the trigger. Stice fled the farm in terror. When he returned four days later he was tortured and shackled. Try as he might, he could not save his son's life.

The boy had been placed in a trailer, where he was suffering daily torture at Ryan's hands. In addition to regular beatings and whippings, the religious leader would spit in the boy's face and flick cigarette ash into his mouth. The end of Luke's young life came when Ryan threw him into a bookcase.

'Yahweh does not want us to take Luke to a hospital,' Ryan announced.

The boy died during the night.

Shot in the face

James Thimm, who was confined to another trailer, was shot in the face by Ryan's son Dennis. He was wasting away, yet he was forced to join Stice in digging Luke's grave.

In the days that followed Thimm was beaten, whipped and sodomized with the handle of a shovel. Throughout all of this misery he asked for Yahweh's forgiveness. His life ended in the hog shed – the building he had come to consider home. After his hands had been tied to an overhead bar with baling wire, Thimm was whipped by Ryan's male followers as their leader watched. When he was taken down, Ryan picked up a Ruger .22 pistol and began shooting off his fingers.

After a break for lunch, Ryan ordered Thimm's murderers to return and resume his torture.

'Yahweh wants me to show you how we skinned people in Vietnam,' he announced.

Using razor blades and a pair of pliers, Ryan proceeded to strip James Thimm's skin from his body, making certain to show his victim each bloody piece of flesh. His son, Dennis, was an eager assistant. They broke Thimm's legs next. Ryan then began kicking his slave in the head, before jumping up and down on the young man's chest. According to Ryan, Yahweh wanted James Thimm dead by dinner time. The deadline was easily met.

On 18 August, the authorities found the grave that contained the bodies of James Thimm and Luke Stice. Ryan, his son Dennis and Timothy Haverkamp, brother of James, were promptly arrested. After being found guilty of second-degree murder, Dennis Ryan and Timothy Haverkamp were sentenced to life imprisonment.

A jury convicted Ryan of first-degree murder on 10 April 1986. As he waited to be sentenced, the cult leader was charged with murdering Luke Stice. In this case, he was found guilty of second-degree murder. Ryan was condemned to die in the electric chair, but moved on to Death Row and spent more than two decades cheating death.

ANTHONY SOWELL
Dead Bodies in the Living Room

I n September 2009 a woman went home with registered sex offender Anthony Sowell for a few drinks. The night soon took a nightmarish turn as a pleasant date turned sour. The victim called the police and reported that Sowell had hit her, choked her and then raped her.

When the police arrived to arrest him, they found the evening's unnerving events were just the tip of the iceberg. Two female corpses greeted them on the living room floor. A skull was hidden in a bucket in the basement. Four more bodies were hidden around the house. Inadvertently, the police had stumbled upon a serial killer who had been operating for years. Sowell was charged with 11 counts of murder and over 70 counts of rape, kidnapping, tampering with evidence, and even the sexual abuse of a corpse.

Weird family life

On Page Avenue, Cleveland, stood a large, 4,000-square-foot house in a rather run-down working-class district slowly but surely sliding into poverty and destitution. This was the scene of the horrible events of Anthony Sowell's childhood. He was born in 1959 to Claudia 'Gertrude' Garrison. Too bad his father, Thomas Sowell, did not stick around long enough to help raise the boy.

Sowell in court

It was far from a normal household. In the house lived Sowell, his mother 'Gertrude', his older sister, Tressa, his brother 'Junior', and seven nieces and nephews who had moved into the house after their mother had died. His mother was not exactly a nurturing presence. She forced Ramona Davis and her twin sister Leona, Sowell's nieces, to strip naked before the other children each day. Then they would be tied to a bannister and whipped with electrical cords. Vindictive Gertrude always found a reason for punishing them, even if she had to make it up.

'It was psycho,' recalled Leona, commenting on the levels of violence in the house. Other siblings were abused, too. Only Sowell, his sister, and his brother were spared.

Sowell was badly affected by the situation, but instead of learning from it he began following his mother's example and taking advantage of others in a very unhealthy way. When he got in trouble, he would blame Leona. She would then be punished for what he had done.

As his nieces began to mature physically, he became obsessed with their bodies and the idea of subjecting them to punishment.

From the age of 11, he began raping his niece. It soon became an everyday occurrence. Sowell was not the only one. His brother Junior and the girl's own brother soon began demanding sexual favours, too, under threat of violence. Leona had tried to report the rapes to the authorities but she found they were unwilling to listen.

When he went to high school, Sowell was tormented for being so quiet and undemonstrative. For some reason, his classmates assumed he lacked sexual experience and teased him about it constantly; he never spoke up about what had been going on at the house. Generally, though, at school he was able to stay out of trouble, but he never did particularly well in his studies.

On leaving school, it seemed that things might be changing for the better. He got out of his mother's house of humiliation and joined the Marines. In September 1981 he married a fellow Marine, Kim Yvette Lawson, who was on a mission to

A county sheriff opens the window in Sowell's bathroom to let in much-needed air

save him from himself – in particular, to help him cut down his excessive drinking.

Unfortunately, the Marines provided Sowell with exactly the training he needed to pursue a campaign of terror. They taught him how to make improvised weapons and to kill with his hands. He also received training as an electrician at Camp Lejeune.

During his seven-year career in the Marines, he picked up a number of awards: a Good Conduct Medal, a Certificate of Commendation, and a Meritorious Mast. His life had not been completely turned around, however.

His wife had married him partly to help him overcome his severe drink problem, but she divorced him the day she left the Marines in 1985, the same year Sowell went back into civilian life. By the mid-1980s, life had deteriorated further in East Cleveland as something far worse than alcohol – crack cocaine – made its debut on the streets.

Sowell's ex-wife Kim died in 1998 having failed entirely in her aim of making him a better man – at the time of her death, Sowell was serving time in an Ohio prison.

Terror on the streets

After his discharge from the Marines, Sowell could not keep out of trouble. Between 1986 and 1989 he was arrested several times, mostly for minor offences – possession of drugs, disorderly conduct, driving under the influence, and public drunkenness.

Around this time women began to go missing in East Cleveland. In May 1988 the strangled corpse of 36-year-old Rosalind Garner was found in her home on Hayden Avenue. Nearly a year later, on 27 February 1989, 27-year-old Carmella Karen Prater was found dead in her home on First Avenue, not far from the location where the earlier victim had been found. Then just one month later, Mary Thomas turned up dead in an abandoned building on First Avenue, with the red ribbon that had been used to strangle her still dangling from her neck.

These cases remain unsolved, but they bore a striking similarity to the murders Sowell would later be convicted for. Mary Cox, one of the women who disappeared, was an acquaintance of Sowell. It is possible that he was responsible for even more killings than the 11 he was eventually convicted for.

In this poisonous climate, the 'Cleveland Strangler', as he became known, began to earn his soubriquet. On 22 July 1989, Sowell met a woman outside a motel on Euclid Avenue. Sowell told her that her boyfriend was waiting for her just around the corner at Sowell's house. When she arrived he choked her and raped her. He tied up her hands with a necktie, looped a belt around her feet and placed a gag in her mouth. When he fell asleep, she managed to escape. A few days later she gave her report to the police. The woman was 21-year-old Melvette Sockwell. She would be the first of Sowell's recognized female victims.

An arrest warrant was issued on 8 December 1989, but he remained free to commit another rape. On 24 June 1990, a 31-year-old woman visited Sowell's house. There Sowell began choking her while describing violent sex acts. He told her 'she was his bitch, and she had better learn to like it'. He raped the woman many times over. She was five months pregnant. Unwilling to face her assailant in court, the woman's name was never revealed.

Sowell pleaded guilty to attempted rape of Sockwell and was sentenced to between five and 15 years in prison. At the trial, his victim stated: 'He choked me real hard because my body started tingling. I thought I was going to die.'

In prison he tried to rehabilitate himself. He attempted to deal with his alcohol problem by signing up with Alcoholics Anonymous and for Adult Children of Alcoholics meetings. He also tried to get help for the the problem that put him behind bars: the impulse to commit sexual assault.

Sowell signed up for sex-offender treatment but stumbled at the first hurdle: he was simply not prepared to admit he was a sex offender. He spent a total of 15 years in the Ohio penitentiary system and was a model prisoner throughout. He took courses with names like 'Living Without Violence' and 'Positive Personal Change'. He cooked and threw barbecues for the other inmates. It was in prison that he finally completed his high-school education, passing the GED in 2002. So when he was released in 2005 it should not come as a surprise that the authorities believed he had been rehabilitated. He was educated, clean and sober. A psychological evaluation in 2005 stated that he was unlikely to rape again.

On the rampage

As a free man he soon reverted to his old ways. Between 2007 and 2009, 11 women were killed by Sowell. Most were African-American women, drug-users and mothers. He began dating women from the troubled neighbourhood of the Mount Pleasant area where he now lived. But on the plus side, he seemed to be developing a more stable relationship with Lori Frazier, the niece of Cleveland's mayor. She moved in with him, unaware of his terrible secrets. The relationship ended abruptly in 2007. Frazier had caught the foul whiff of something nasty in his house. Sowell claimed it came from the sausage factory across the road.

The truth was far more chilling. It was the stench of the dead bodies that he had hidden around his home. One of the first victims to be discovered was Crystal Dozier who'd gone missing in May 2007. To maintain his supply of prey, Sowell had joined a sex fetish website, Alt.com. His profile stated: 'If your [sic] submissive and like to please, then this master wants to talk to you.' In 2008 and 2009 more women would disappear.

On 21 April 2009, Tanja Doss visited Sowell and was slapped, choked and forced to strip naked. On 22 September, he attacked another woman who was visiting him, whose name has never been released. He raped her while tightening an electrical cord around her neck until she passed out. Unlike many of Sowell's victims, she was not afraid to go to the police. After most of his attacks, he acted as if nothing had happened. He offered some of his victims food and money and escorted them calmly out of the door. But the majority never left the house on Imperial Avenue.

When the police arrived to arrest him, they found an array of bodies hidden within. Two corpses were in plain view on the living room floor. A skull was found in a bucket in the basement. Shallow graves had been dug in the backyard and bodies left in crawl spaces. In total there were 11 bodies hidden around the house.

Most had been strangled. The interrogation of Sowell by Detectives Lem Griffin and Melvin Smith on 31 October 2009 left little room for doubt:

'Did you strangle these girls?''That's what I did. I think with just my hands.'

On hearing the news about Sowell, Regina Woodland, a woman who lived nearby, asked: 'What kind of man was this? He couldn't have been human.'

By the time of his second conviction in court there were 11 bodies to Sowell's name along with countless rapes and kidnappings. In 2005, the authorities made the mistake of releasing him back into the world, but not this time. On 10 August 2011, Sowell was sentenced to death.

FRED AND ROSEMARY WEST
The Builder's Torture Chamber

red West spent a lot of his spare time renovating 25 Cromwell Street, Gloucester, the house he shared with his wife Rosemary. But then he was a builder. So when a mechanical digger showed up on 24 February 1994, his neighbours would not have been unduly surprised. But this wasn't just another of Fred's projects – the digger had been brought in by the local police force. They had hired the machine in an attempt to solve an old mystery. Seven years earlier, Fred and Rosemary's 16-year-old daughter had gone missing. Acting on a tip, the Gloucester police now had reason to believe that the girl's body would be found buried in the Wests' back garden.

And it was – along with the remains of two other young females. The search then moved inside the West home. Five more corpses were found underneath the cellar floor, with a sixth hidden under the linoleum-covered floorboards in the bathroom. The sudden police activity at the Wests' home was a shock to many of their neighbours. Fred was so friendly, according to one of his neighbours.

'He was always the kind of guy who would say, "Come on in." He'd say, "Have a cup of tea."'

But to others in the area, 25 Cromwell Street was more than just a busy family home. Rosemary was a prostitute who entertained male clients at her husband's bidding. The first-floor brothel that Fred had fashioned for Rosemary was not just a source of income. It also enabled the couple to explore their fantasies. Fred's videotaped recordings of Rosemary's encounters formed just a small part of his vast collection. Violence, rape, incest, torture, voyeurism and paedophilia were everyday occurrences at 25 Cromwell Street, and all of it had been carefully filmed by Fred.

Depraved

Couples who rape, torture and murder their victims are sadly not rare. But even in this depraved company the Wests stand out. They met on 29 November 1968, Rosemary's 15th birthday. Fred was 27 years old and not much of a catch. Born on 29 September 1941 to a couple of farm labourers, he received only a rudimentary education. His employment record only merits attention because he ran over and killed a 4-year-old boy when he was working as an ice-cream salesman.

Fred was already divorced from Catherine (Rena) Costello by the time he met Rosemary. Rena was pregnant by another man

Violence, rape, incest, torture, voyeurism and paedophilia were all part of a normal day for the Wests

when she married Fred, but he accepted her child, Charmaine, as his own. She later gave birth to Anna Marie, who really was Fred's child. During this time the couple befriended Anne McFall, who started living with Fred when Rena left him.

Anne began to put pressure on Fred when she became pregnant, but she paid for it with her life, because she disappeared in August 1967.

There was also the matter of Fred's criminal record. He had twice been found guilty of petty theft and at the age of 20 he had been convicted of having sex with a 13-year-old girl.

What she knew of Fred's troubled history did not bother young Rosemary Letts. It was not that her background was much better. Her mother suffered from extreme depression, while her father regularly beat his wife and children. Rosemary was far from intelligent – in fact, she was known as 'Dozy Rosie' at school. Her nickname was by no means a term of affection, because she had no real friends and she passed unnoticed in the hallways.

Fred's interest meant a great deal to a girl like Rosemary, who suffered from low self-esteem, and it also allowed her to escape a dreadful family situation.

Prison

Rosemary moved in with Fred on her 16th birthday, which was the anniversary of their first meeting. The couple's first home together was a caravan. Fred supported them through odd jobs and theft. Not long afterwards the couple moved to a two-storey home on Gloucester's Midland Road, where they welcomed the birth of their first child, Heather – the girl whose body would one day be dug up from the Wests' back garden.

Just after Heather's birth, Fred was sent to prison for theft.

He left his 8-year-old stepdaughter Charmaine in Rosemary's care while he was away, but when he returned six months later Rosemary had killed her. He covered the murder up by burying the girl's corpse underneath the kitchen floor, but first of all he cut off her fingers and toes. When Rena, Fred's ex-wife, came looking for Charmaine, she too was killed.

Fred and Rosemary were married on 29 January 1972. The bride was pregnant with her second child, but whether or not Fred was the father is a matter for conjecture. Rosemary had been entertaining male clients in and around Gloucester for some months and she continued to do so when she was pregnant. However, Fred encouraged his new wife's occupation, to the extent that he watched through a peephole.

Rosemary's earnings went a long way towards funding the purchase of 25 Cromwell Street, the couple's home from 1972 onwards. Fred was quite taken with his new home.

It was much larger for a start, but what really attracted him was the cellar. He set about creating a soundproof 'Torture Chamber', in which a number of girls and women would later be victimized.

The couple's first victim was 8-year-old Anna Marie, Fred's daughter by Rena. Fred raped her as Rosemary held her down. These assaults lasted throughout the remainder of the girl's childhood and would continue into her adult years. By the end of 1972 Fred and Rosemary were ready to invite potential victims into their lair. Seventeen-year-old Caroline Owens was the first to be lured in. The unsuspecting girl thought she had been hired as the Wests' nanny, but Fred and Rosemary clearly had other plans. Both of them made overt advances, which disgusted Caroline. When she attempted to leave, they forced her downstairs to the torture chamber. Her clothes were stripped off and she was raped, after which Fred threatened to kill her.

Rape charge

Fred might have succeeded in keeping Caroline quiet but he could not silence her mother. When she noticed her daughter's bruises she called the police. At the beginning of 1973, Fred and Rosemary were summoned to appear in court on a rape charge, but they were lucky on that occasion – Caroline could not face the ordeal of giving evidence. As a result, the couple escaped jail.

After pleading guilty to a reduced charge of indecent assault, they were merely fined £100 between them.

With Caroline out of the picture, Fred and Rosemary brought in a new person to care for their children. No one knows what happened between 21-year-old Lynda Gough and the depraved couple, but her body was later found in the back garden with the others.

Lynda's murder appeared to signal a change of direction for the Wests. One murder followed another in quick succession. In November 1973 the Wests abducted, raped and strangled 15-year-old student Carol Ann Cooper as she was walking home from a cinema. They killed another student, Lucy Partington, a month later. A cousin of novelist Martin Amis, it is thought that she was kept alive for several days before meeting her end.

The Wests' killing spree came to a halt after the August 1979 murder of a 17-year-old runaway named Alison Chambers. By this time, Fred and Rosemary had killed a total of eleven girls and women – nine of whom had been murdered at 25 Cromwell Street. No one knows why the murders stopped.

Perhaps it was because the couple had decided to take in

boarders. There is a theory that the Wests did not change their behaviour at all. Instead, they might have found a better way of hiding the evidence of their killings.

Perversions

Fred and Rosemary's last known murder was that of their daughter Heather. The unfortunate girl came into the firing line when her sister Anna Marie left 25 Cromwell Street. Fred then made his second eldest daughter the focus of his perversions. When Heather resisted her father's advances, she was killed by Rosemary. Although Fred and Rosemary told their children that Heather had run off, the couple would also warn them that any bad behaviour would lead them to be buried in the back garden, just like Heather.

It wasn't until 1992, a quarter-century after Fred had killed his first victim, Anna Fall, that the Wests faced the beginning of the end. The couple probably did not recognize it at first. In fact,

After the discovery of the first body, the Wests were taken into custody

for a time it appeared as if they had once again managed to elude the authorities.

That May, Fred filmed himself as he raped one of his daughters. When the girl told a friend, her story spread to the Gloucester police. Search warrant in hand, they showed up on Fred's doorstep. After searching 25 Cromwell Street they arrested Fred, charging him with the rape and sodomy of a minor. Rose was accused of assisting in the assault. Though the case collapsed, the detectives noticed something curious about the videotapes they had seized during their investigation – Heather was missing.

Their suspicions of foul play were strengthened when Anna Marie told them about the abuse she had suffered while she had been growing up in the West household. When she went on to mention the curious disappearances of Heather and Charmaine, the alarm bells rang non-stop.

Despite his troubles with the law and the accusations of sexual assault that had been levelled at him over the years, Fred maintained his innocence. As the mechanical digger began to excavate the Wests' garden on that February day in 1994, he told the police that Heather was a problem child who had run away with her lesbian lover. If something unfortunate had happened to Heather, he said, it most probably would have been the result of her involvement with a drug-smuggling ring.

After the discovery of the first decapitated and dismembered body, Fred and Rosemary were taken into custody. The next morning, Fred admitted to murdering the girls and women whose remains had been found at 25 Cromwell Street. But he did not admit to the rapes. He tried to make it appear that his victims had been willing participants in the sexual activities that had preceded their deaths. An indignant Fred chastised his interrogators.

'You've even got the killing wrong. You're trying to make out I just went and blatantly killed somebody. No, nobody went through hell. Enjoyment turned into disaster, that's what happened – most of it anyway.'

Apportioning the blame

Fred did his best to protect Rosemary from prosecution by maintaining that she had not been involved in the murders. But he did not know that Rosemary had already cut him loose. While he was trying to protect her, she was doing her level best to shift all of the responsibility on to his shoulders. If anything, Rosemary said, she was a victim.

However, the stories she told were flawed and unconvincing. At the end of the day, 40-year-old Rosemary West was still 'Dozy Rosie'.

Rosemary kept the act up even during the couple's joint hearing. Although this would be the last time they would ever lay eyes on one another, she pulled away from her husband, telling those in attendance that he made her sick.

On 13 December 1994, Fred was formally charged with 12 counts of murder. Nineteen days later he was found hanging in his cell.

Rosemary had to wait another ten months for her trial. When the day arrived, she was found guilty of ten counts of murder. She received a life sentence for each crime.

In one of the last letters Rosemary received from Fred, he expressed his undying love. Then he said, 'You will always be Mrs West, all over the world.'

And so she remains.

STEVE WRIGHT
The Moving Chamber

Steven Gerald James Wright was an organized and calculating killer, whose car was a mobile death chamber. His victims, all prostitutes, entered the vehicle with little hesitation, even though they were aware that a serial killer was on the prowl. A 19-year-old named Tania Nicol was the first to go missing. She disappeared on 30 October 2006, but her mother did not report her absence until two days later. Tania was a student at Chantry High School, but she also worked as a prostitute using the alias 'Chantelle'. In the weeks leading up to her disappearance, she had been walking the streets to support her addiction to heroin and crack cocaine. Her parents knew nothing about her drug habit or her adopted occupation. In fact, Tania's mother thought her daughter worked at a hairdressing salon.

Another teenage runaway, perhaps? The police were not so sure. According to the records, her mobile phone had shown no activity since she had been reported missing.

Steve Wright was an organized and calculating killer who preyed on prostitutes

Seventeen days later, in the early hours of 15 November, Gemma Adams also went missing. A heroin addict like Tania, she too had been working as a prostitute. The police learned of the young woman's disappearance from her boyfriend, Jon Simpson, with whom she had been for ten of her 25 years. The recent past had not been the best of times for the couple. Gemma's progression from marijuana to heroin had resulted in her being fired from her job at an insurance firm. What is more, she cut herself off from her parents and her sister when they tried to get her into a rehabilitation clinic.

Naked body

Following this second disappearance, the police began stopping motorists in the city's small red light district. Over 500 cars were stopped and 2,000 people were questioned, yet the investigation yielded no information. This all changed on the morning of 2 December, when Gemma's naked body was discovered by a park worker. The location, Belstead Brook, would prove to be a challenge to the forensic investigators, who recognized that the swift-moving water would almost certainly have washed away any fibres, hair or DNA.

Undaunted, the team of policemen doggedly searched the area. On the sixth day they found Tania's submerged, naked body 3 km (2 miles) downstream.

The double murder inquiry was less than 48 hours old when the body of a third prostitute was discovered. The news came as a shock, because no one had reported the victim missing.

She was Anneli Alderton, a 24-year-old who had once entertained dreams of becoming a model. While she certainly had the looks, she had been dependent on drugs during the eight years that led to her death. At the time of her death, the mother of one was three months pregnant.

The killer must have been bold because the prostitute had gone missing when there was a noticeably heightened police presence in Ipswich's red-light district. Was the murderer taunting the police? The way in which Anneli's body had been left indicated that this was so. She was found in a secluded wood on the outskirts of Ipswich, less than 16 km (10 miles) from where she had plied her trade. Like the other two victims, her body was naked.

However, that was where the similarities ended. Anneli had been found on dry land and her killer had taken a good deal of time to arrange the body in the shape of a cross.

'She was pristine, she looked like an angel,' said one detective.

The location of the corpse gave the police an advantage that they had not had with the other victims. For the first time they were looking at the possibility of harvesting a significant amount of forensic evidence from the body and the surrounding area.

Now that the bodies of three Ipswich prostitutes had been found in just six days, it was clear that a serial killer was on the prowl in the seamier part of the city. Yet prostitutes continued to walk the streets of the red-light district. The police issued constant warnings, but they were ignored – the girls needed money to feed their drugs habits.

Shape of the cross

Less than 48 hours later, on 12 December, another body was found just metres off the busy Old Felixstowe Road. Again, the victim had been arranged in the shape of a cross. At 29 years of age, Annette Nicholls would be the oldest of all the victims.

Annette was a very attractive woman who had suffered a rough upbringing. She nearly managed to rise above her disadvantaged childhood by studying to be a beautician, but then she succumbed to heroin addiction.

All available police officers were dispatched to the area and a helicopter was brought in to film the scene from the air. As the camera panned along the roadside a second body came into view. The fifth victim, Paula Clennell, was a 24-year-old drug addict and mother of three. Paula had been walking the streets for years.

Indeed, she had continued to do so even in the knowledge that there was a prostitute killer on the loose. Just six days before she vanished, Paula had been interviewed by a local television journalist. The young woman admitted that she was 'a bit wary about getting into cars', but she said that she needed the money. There was something markedly different about Paula's body. She was not carefully laid out in a cruciform position – in fact, it appeared that no care had been taken at all. The corpse had simply been dumped.

More than 300 local police officers were now working overtime on the case, with assistance from a further 500 throughout the country. Almost immediately, there appeared to be a breakthrough. A 37-year-old supermarket worker was taken into custody after he had told a newspaper that he knew all five women. Under questioning from the police, the man further revealed that he could offer no alibi for the evenings on which the victims had gone missing.

As police investigators searched the supermarket worker's home, other officers managed to find traces of DNA on the bodies of the three women who had been found on land. Such extraordinarily small amounts were present that there was little hope that the samples would prove useful. And yet the forensics team managed to prove that the DNA that had been found on all three bodies had come from the same person.

Lucky break

When the samples were checked against the United Kingdom National DNA Database, the police were treated to another lucky break. The DNA belonged to a 48-year-old forklift operator named Steve Wright – a man who had not even been considered as a suspect. Wright might not have been on the investigators' radar, but they did have his name. He had been stopped and questioned during the road checks that had taken place earlier in the month. In the pre-dawn hours of 19 December, one week after the final bodies were found, Wright was removed from his house in handcuffs.

But who was Steve Wright? Police had already begun looking into his background. Steven Gerald James Wright, the man who would go down in history as 'the Suffolk Strangler' and 'the Ipswich Ripper', had been born on 24 April 1958 in the Norfolk village of Erpingham. As the son of a military man, he had spent his early years in Malta and Singapore. Beaten by his father, his unhappy childhood was made all the worse at the age of 8, when his mother abandoned the family. Wright and his three siblings remained with their father and were later joined by a stepmother and two more children.

Wright's physically abusive father failed to provide his son with any guidance, so he never seemed to find his footing in life. Sailor, ship's steward, barman, lorry driver, he moved from one job to the next. Women came and went in much the same way.

Wright's first marriage, in 1978, lasted nine years and produced a son. His second, which began just weeks after the divorce, was over within 11 months. A Thai woman said that she had married Wright in 1999, but her claim was never substantiated. There were many other women in his life, including Sarah Whiteley, who gave birth to his daughter in 1992.

In 2001 he met his final partner, Pamela Wright. Quite by chance he shared his surname with her.

In October 2004, just weeks before Tania Nicol went missing, the couple moved to a rented flat at 79 London Road. It was one of the few streets that make up Ipswich's red-light district. Prior to his arrest, Wright had only had one brush with the law. This was while he was working as a hotel barman. He had been caught stealing £80 from the till to pay off his gambling debts. A petty crime, it is true, but it had been enough to get his DNA entered on to the national database.

Armed with the DNA evidence, the police charged Wright with the murders of the five dead prostitutes. What did Wright have to say about the presence of his DNA? The only words he uttered during the hours of intense interrogation were 'No comment'.

Flakes of blood

Wright's trial was set for January 2008. In the meantime, the police would work at gathering evidence. His Ford Mondeo was their primary focus.

CCTV cameras had filmed Gemma getting into the vehicle on the night that she had disappeared. Not only that, the forklift driver's new neighbours had told the police that he continually cleaned the vehicle, sometimes in the early hours of the morning.

Inside the foot well, they found two fake fur fibres that exactly matched the ones on Annette Nicholls' naked body. Some small flakes of blood on the back seat matched Paula Clennell's DNA and fibres from the Mondeo's carpet were found in Tania Nicol's hair. That proved that her head had been in contact with the floor well of the car at some point.

On the first day of his trial, 14 January 2008, Wright was charged with the murder of the five women. He pleaded not guilty, although he admitted that he frequented prostitutes. Annette had been in his car, he said, but he had done nothing more than have sex with her on the back seat. Tania had also been in the Mondeo, but only briefly – her acne had turned him off.

The cold, self-assured Wright eventually began to crumble under the persistent questioning of the prosecution, who had nothing more than a few flakes of blood, some small traces of DNA and several stray fibres to work with. H. H. Holmes' Murder Castle, David Parker Ray's trailer or the pot on Joachim Kroll's stove had provided the authorities with much more in the way of evidence. But Steve Wright had run up against the 21st century.

On 21 February, it took a jury of nine men and three women just eight hours to find Wright guilty on all five counts of murder. He received a life sentence.

INDEX

BIBLIOGRAPHY

Esther Adderley. 'How Police Closed the Net on Steve Wright.' *The Guardian*, 21 February 2006.

Philip Delves Broughton. 'Killer "Gave Victim's Daughter to Brother."' *The Telegraph*, 26 August 2000.

Annemie Bulté, Douglas de Conick & Marie-Jeanne van Heeswyck. *Les Dossiers X: ce que la Belgique ne devait pas Savoir sur l'affaire Dutroux*. Brussels: Epo, 1999.

Rod Colvin. *Evil Harvest: The Shocking True Story of Cult Murder in the American Heartland*. New York: Bantam, 1992.

Kate Connolly. 'Fritzl's Troubled Childhood Analysed in Court.' *The Guardian*, 18 March 2009.

'Josef Fritzl Trial: "She Spent the First Five Years Entirely Alone. He Hardly Ever Spoke to Her."' *The Guardian*, 19 March 2009.

'Light Out. Rape. Light On. Rape. In Front of the Children. Birth. Death. Rape.' *The Guardian*, 17 March 2009.

'Power-hungry Unloved Son Who was "Born to Rape". Birth. Death. Rape.' *The Guardian*, 19 March 2009.

& Helen Pidd. 'Josef Fritzl Sentenced to Life in Psychiatric Institution.' *The Guardian*, 19 March 2009.

& Helen Pidd. 'Josef Fritzl Trial: Engineer Pleads Guilty Over Baby's Death in Austrian Cellar.' *The Guardian*, 18 March 2009.

Oliver Cyriax. *Crime: An Encyclopedia*. London: Andre Deutsch, 1993.

Lionel Dahmer. *A Father's Story*. New York: Morrow, 1994.

John Douglas. *Anyone You Want Me to Be: A True Story of Sex and Death on the Internet*. New York: Scribner, 2003.

Kevin Dwyer & Juré Fiorillo. *True Stories of Law and Order: Special Victims Unit*. New York: Berkley, 2007.

John Eddowes. *The Two Killers of Rillington Place*. New York: Little, Brown, 1994.

Vivien Encel and Alan Sharpe. *Murder! 25 True Australian Crimes*, Sydney. Kingsclear, 1997.

Ken Englande. *Cellar of Horror: The Story of Gary Heidnik*. New York: St Martins, 1989.

Jim Fielder. *Slow Death*. New York: Pinnacle, 2003.

Mike Fish. 'Chamber of Horrors.' *The Syracuse Post-Standard*, 4 May 2003.

& Mike McAndrew. 'Out of Bunker and Into Karaoke Bar.' *The Syracuse Post-Standard*, 24 April 2003.

David Frasier. *Murder Cases of the Twentieth Century*. Jefferson, NC: McFarland, 1996.

Jennifer Furio. *Team Killers: A Comparative Study of Collaborative Criminals*. New York: Algora, 2001.

Dirk Cameron Gibson. *Clues from Killers: Serial Murder and Crime Scene Messages*. Santa Barbara, CA: Greenwood, 2004.

John Glatt. *Cries in the Desert: The Shocking True Story of a Sadistic Torturer*. New York: St Martin's, 2002.

Allan Hall and Michael Leidig. *Girl in the Cellar: The Natascha Kampusch Story*. New York: HarperCollins, 2007.

Eric Hickey. *Serial Murderers and Their Victims*, 3rd ed. Belmont, CA: Wadsworth, 1998.

Martin Hintz. *Got Murder?: The Shocking Story of Wisconsin's Notorious Killers*. Boulder, CO: Trails, 2007.

Robert J. Hoshowsky. *Unsolved: True Canadian Cold Cases*. Toronto: Dundurn, 2010.

'Ipswich Prostitute Murders: the Victims.' *The Telegraph*, 21 February 2008.

Terry J. Hughes. 'Police Seek Victims from Torture Photos.' *The St Louis Post-Dispatch*, 7 April 1988.

Tom Jackman and Troy Cole. *Rites of Burial: The Shocking True Crime Account of Robert Berdella, the Butcher of Kansas City, Missouri*. New York: Pinnacle, 1992.

Andrew Jacobs. 'Man Gets 18 Years to Life For Holding Women Captive.' *The New York Times*, 16 July 2003.

—'Town Loner Charged in Chilling Case of Sexual Captivity,' *The New York Times*, 19 April 2003.

Natascha Kampusch. *3096 Days*. London: Penguin, 2010.

Ludovic Kennedy. *Ten Rillington Place*. New York: Simon & Schuster, 1961.

Paul B. Kidd. *Australia's Serial Killers: The Definitive History of Serial Multicide in Australia*. Sydney: Pan Macmillan, Sydney, 2000.

&. *Never To Be Released*. Sydney: Pan Macmillan, 1993.

Brian Lane & Wilfred Gregg. *The Encyclopedia of Serial Killers*. New York: Berkley, 1995.

Erik Larson. *Devil in the White City: Murder, Magic, and Madness at the Fair that Changed America*. New York: Crown, 2003.

Don Lasseter. *Die for Me: The Terrifying True Story of the Charles Ng/Leonard Lake Torture Murders*. New York: Pinnacle, 2000.

Herwig Lerouge. *Le Dossier Nihoul: les enjeux du process Dutroux*. Brussels: Epo, 2004.

Paul Lewis. 'Police Warn Prostitutes to Stay off the Streets.' *The Guardian*, 12 December 2006.

Elliott Leyton. *Hunting Humans: The Rise of the Modern Multiple Murderer*. Toronto: McClelland & Stewart, 1995.

Clifford L. Linedecker. *The Man Who Killed Boys*. New York: St Martin's, 1994.

Brian Marriner. *A New Century of Sex Killers*. London: Pan, 2003.

—. *She Must Have Known: The Trial of Rosemary West*. London: Corgi, 1996.

Moira Martingale. *Cannibal Killers: The History of Impossible Murders*. New York: Carroll & Graf, 1993.

Mike McAndrew & Mike Fish. 'John T. Jamleske: The Unfolding Story.' *The Syracuse Post-Standard*, 18 May 2003.

Christine McGuire & Carla Norton. *Perfect Victim: The True Story of the Girl in the Box by the D.A. Who Prosecuted her Captor*. New York: Dell, 1989.

Michael Musto. 'NY Mirror.' *The Village Voice*, 26 March 2002.

Phillippe Naughton. 'Suffolk Strangler Steve Wright Jailed for "Whole Life Term."' *The Times*, 22 February 2008.

—& Jenny Percival. 'Two More Women Found Dead Near Ipswich.' *The Times*, 12 December 2006.

Jim O'Hara. 'Jamelske Gets 18 to Life.' *The Syracuse Post-Standard*, 15 July 2003.

—. 'Jamelske On Growing Up, Marriage, Sex and Cruisin'.' *The Syracuse Post-Standard*, 17 July 2003.

Sean O'Neill. 'He Was Rude and Aggressive, but No One's Idea of a Killer.' *The Times*, 22 February 2008.

Frank Owen. *Clubland: The Fabulous Rise and Murderous Fall of Club Culture*. New York: Broadway, 2004.

Christine Quigley. *The Corpse: A History*. Jefferson, NC: McFarland, 2005.

Fred Rosen. *Blood Crimes: The Pennsylvania Skinhead Murders*. New York: Kensington, 1996.

—. *The Historical Atlas of American Crime*. New York: Facts on File, 2005.

Ann Rule. *Lust Killer*. New York: Signet, 1988.

Harold Schechter. *Depraved: The Shocking True Story of America's First Serial Killer*. New York: Pocket, 1994.

—. *Deviant: The Shocking True Story of Ed Gein, the Original Psycho*. New York: Pocket, 1998.

—. *The Serial Killer Files: The Who, What, Where, How, and Why of the World's Most Terrifying Murderers*. New York: Ballantine, 2003.

— & David Everitt. *The A-Z Encyclopedia of Serial Killers*. New York: Pocket, 1996.

Anne E. Schwartz. *The Man Who Could Not Kill Enough: The Secret Murders of Milwaukee's Jeffrey Dahmer*. New York: Citadel, 1992.

Alan Sharpe & Vivien Encel. *Murder!: 25 True Australian Crimes*. Sydney: Kingsclear, 1997.

Suzanne Smalley & Seth Mnookin. 'A House of Horrors,' *Newsweek*, 5 May 2003.

Greg Smith. 'Sex-Slay Suspect's Secret Life.' *The New York Daily News*, 11 June 2000.

James St James. *Disco Bloodbath: A Fabulous But True Tale of Murder in Clubland*. New York: Simon & Schuster, 1999.

Howard Sounes. *Fred and Rose*. London: Warner Books, 1995.

David Thigpen. 'The Bodies in the Barrels.' *Time*, 19 June 2000.

'Two Skinhead Brothers Charged With Killing Family Members.' *The New York Times*, 3 March 1995.

Jo Thomas. 'Police Identify 2nd of 5 Bodies in Barrels on Kansas Farm.' *The New York Times*, 13 June 2000.

—& Robert D. McFadden. 'Man's Farm Reveals Unsavory Secret.' *The New York Times*, 9 June 2000.

Peter Vronsky. *Serial Killers*. New York: Berkley, 2004.

Geoffrey Wansell. *The Life of Frederick West*. London: Headline, 1996.

Cyril Wecht & Greg Saitz with Mark Curriden. *Mortal Evidence: The Forensics Behind Nine Shocking Cases*, Amherst, NY: Prometheus, 2003.

Colin Wilson. *The Corpse Garden: The Crimes of Fred and Rose West*. London: True Crime Library, 1998.

— & Donald Seaman. *The Serial Killers: A Study in the Psychology of Violence*. London: Allen, 1990.

Rogers Worthington. 'House of Horrors Shocks Residents of a Quiet Neighborhood.' *The Chicago Tribune*, 31 July 1988.